Growing Up in the Last Small Town

A West Virginia Memoir

Growing Up in the
Last Small Town

A West Virginia Memoir

Bob Barnett

JESSE STUART
FOUNDATION

ISBN 1-931672-59-8

Book & Cover Design by

Suzanna & Anthony Stephens
designs-on-you.net

Published by

Jesse Stuart Foundation
1645 Winchester Avenue • P.O. Box 669
Ashland, Kentucky 41101-0669
(606) 326-1667
JSFBOOKS.com

To Liz

who is always there

with love when I need help

Versions of the following previously published articles appear in this work. Used with permission.

⟶

"When the Big Green Rolled," *Goldenseal Magazine*, spring 2005, 9 - 17.

"The Wall of China: Remembering the World's Greatest Dump," *Goldenseal Magazine*, spring 1992, 17 - 33.

"Friday Night Rites: High School Football in the Northern Panhandle," *Goldenseal Magazine*, fall, 1989, 55 - 59. Reprinted in the Wheeling News-Register October 17, 1991.

"Tickets to the Series," in *The Ol' Ballgame*, Tracy Cartmell, ed., Harrisburg: PA: Stackpole Press, 1990, 89 - 91.

Co-authored with Lysbeth A. Barnett. "Spring Baseball," *Goldenseal Magazine*, spring 1984, 8.

Table of Contents

Acknowledgments

I owe a debt of gratitude to the Jesse Stuart Foundation and specifically to James Gifford, the CEO and Senior Editor, who has always been extremely supportive of my writing. Suzanna and Anthony Stephens of *Designs on You!*, talented designers and editors who are easy to work with, provided the design of the book.

Michele Schiavone who provided the early editing and Tina Holmes who provided the semifinal editing were always encouraging and both provided helpful suggestions during the writing process. However, Liz Barnett, who was, is, and always will be, my best editor enhanced the final manuscript immeasurably. Mary Brandal, Megan Barnett, Alexis Sergi, Jean Verner, Jim Barnett, Hil Barnett, David Nurmi, Denise May, Ed LaNeve, Joseph Wells III, Sarah Webster Vodrey, and Jane Powell all read chapters and provided helpful comments and criticism.

John and Joby Laneve, Ron LaNeve, Jim McDevitt, and Norm Six were extremely helpful with the Championship Season Chapter. Opal Lantz and Clarence L. Barnett provided inside information for the first chapter. Ed Peters had a wealth of information for the baseball chapter. David Nurmi provided expert information for the Epilog. Joseph Wells III provided a gracious and candid interview about his family and the history of The Homer Laughlin China Company.

Dan Williams of The Homer Laughlin China Company and Tamara Pettit of Mountaineer Casino Racetrack & Resort both provided historical information and allowed me access to their company's picture archives.

Mary Brandal, the LaNeve family, particularly Ron LaNeve, and Joan LaNeve Martin, Marilyn Gibas, Larry Hutton, and Bob Shenton all shared their family histories with me. Bob and Marilyn were always only a phone call away when I needed local fact checking or to review my fuzzy memories. Plus many others who are recognized in the Sources section were kind enough to share their memories with me.

The pictures in this book make the 1950s come alive. Special thanks go to Ruth Fuller who graciously let me use her Newell High School Yearbooks and her personal pictures. Cindy Goad, Mary Brandal, Jim Barnett, Jane Powell, Joby Laneve, George Hines, Colleen Waggle, Norm Six, The Tri-State Genealogical & Historical Society, the East Liverpool Historical Society, the Hancock County Historical Society, the Museum of Ceramics, *Goldenseal Magazine*, and *The Brooke Review,* were all more than gracious in providing the use of their pictures. When the source is not identified the picture is from our family collection.

Research facilities were provided by the Carnegie Library of East Liverpool, the Lynn Murray Library of Chester, the Sarasota County Library, The Tri-State Genealogical & Historical Society, the Hancock County Historical Society, and the Marshall University Library.

Finally, special thanks go to Phyllis Koppel and the Memoir Writing Group at the Meadows in Sarasota, Florida. They were critical readers but more importantly I needed them as friends who at least pretended to like my writing and always encouraged me to keep at the task. Their support was a ray of light when the writing tunnel often seemed dark and gloomy.

Writing a book is never easy, but with the help of the people of Newell, my family, my friends, both old and new, and the Jesse Stuart Foundation the task was accomplished and you now have the book in your hands.

Preface

Once small towns were local. Local people owned corner grocery stores, diners and shops that existed only in your town. Every small town had its own high school. We watched our town teams play and had our own heroes. Families lived in the same town for generations, sometimes in the same house. Sons grew up to work on the same family farms and local industries as their fathers. We stayed at home and knew little beyond its boundaries. Towns a mile away seemed distant and a little strange; those fifty miles away were foreign to us. This was home.

There are still little towns, but they are tied to a national culture in a way that small towns never were. The world has come into today's little towns through television and the internet, on the interstates, with the McDonalds and Wal-Marts; and the unique character of each small town has vanished. The world has come into each little town as its local industries crumbled, its schools were consolidated and its families scattered; and the bonds of community that once held us close have stretched and weakened. The small towns of the thirties, forties, and fifties, are gone. My generation was the last to know what it meant to grow up in a small town.

When I was growing up my mom called Newell, West Virginia a one-horse town. I was offended. True, Newell was small. In 1950, it had slightly more than 2,000 residents and really was not a town because it was not incorporated. But, I thought Newell was wonderful. We had the Waterford Park racetrack, The Homer Laughlin China Company, the largest pottery in the world, and had the world's greatest dump located right in the middle of town. Newell High School had championship basketball and baseball teams. To me, Newell was then, and will ever be, number one. I loved that town.

I wasn't alone. All over America people loved their small towns and the lives they lived there. As soon as World War II was over, my wife's uncle, George Scott, my father, and my four uncles all wanted to return to the Ohio Valley and work in the mill. I often wondered why they were so eager to leave some of the wonderful places like Hawaii, Washington, D.C., or Philadelphia and come back to these little Ohio Valley industrial towns like Chester, Weirton, Follansbee, and yes, Newell. The mills and factories made the towns dirty, the people who lived there were largely uneducated, the towns were pretty much devoid of culture, and life was not very progressive.

They all wanted to come back because it was home, where they had grown up, where their relatives were, and where their friends still lived. The idea of home resonates in the hearts of all Appalachians. The upper Ohio Valley with the mighty Ohio River, rugged hills, and smokestack industries captured the hearts of Appalachians just as strongly as the rocky farms and the coal mines of the southern mountains.

Small towns in postwar America represented family and friends, security, and a chance to work in the mill and capture a part of the American dream. Best of all, this was all done among people you had known all of your life. You went to the same schools,

Postcard view of the Newell Park, c. 1909. (Courtesy of Fred and Colleen Waggle, The Tri-State Genealogical & Historical Society)

shopped in the same stores, drank in the same bars, and worshiped in the same churches. You knew the life stories of everyone in the town and you took care of one another. I was reared by people who believed in the rightness of small town life. They believed big cities were cold and dangerous, and farms too isolated. The best life, they believed, was located in the main streets of small town America.

In the 1950s the seeds of change that were planted in the post World War II period began to grow and the world began to change. The large mills that served as the main employers in small towns began to struggle. Many closed their doors, forcing people to leave the area to find jobs. Television quickly changed the entertainment habits in America. Families stayed home instead of going out to community activities, and they abandoned the time honored tradition of sitting on their front porches on warm summer evenings. Worst of all, school consolidation, which began at this time, ended up tearing the hearts out of small towns by taking their high schools.

This book is about me, because it is a memoir; however, I also attempt to chronicle the response of people—specifically the people of Newell—as they tried to grasp the changing landscape of a postwar, modern America. It is a story of a town and a time. It is the story of growing up in Newell, West Virginia, a small pottery town on the margins of the Appalachians—the last small town in America.

Chapter 1
Home Place and Family

I came by my love of home place and family through my Appalachian roots. My mother and father were very Appalachian even before the term and region were widely recognized. They shared an intense love of their home place, Follansbee, West Virginia and their extended family that would influence their entire lives and also mine.

Follansbee, where my parents grew up and I spent the first seven years of my life, was a steel mill town with a population of 4,834 located on the Ohio River in the northern panhandle of West Virginia. The town, built at the turn of the century around the Follansbee Brothers Steel Company, was long and skinny—fitting into the narrow river valley between the mill on the riverbank and the hills that rose steeply from the valley floor. Follansbee was divided into three parts. The south end of town was where the Italians lived. They had family names like Ciccolella, Iacoune, Sacripanti, Ciccherillo, and Sisinni. Hundreds of immigrants had been recruited from Italy to work in the mill. The new immigrants clustered in the lower end of town where the Garibaldi and Italian Clubs where located and where Italian men drank red wine and smoked thin cigars while they played bocce.

The middle part of Follansbee, where my father grew up, had two streets on the valley floor jammed against the mill and three streets that clung to the side of a hill so steep that houses could be built only on the upper side of the street. Three sets of very steep steps led up the steep hillside from St. Anthony's Catholic Church and grade school so that the mill workers could walk directly to work and avoid the longer route down the winding streets. The middle part of town housed mill workers with names like Barnett, Verner, and Carey; and the established Italian families with names like Tabbi, Ficca, and Anastasio.

My mother's family lived in the Orchard section of town where the park, swimming pool, and high school were located. Tree lined streets shaded the homes of professional people, mill foremen, and the rising working class. With names like Anderson, Mahan, Hume, Lantz, and Schwertfeger, they were for the most part old stock Americans who traced their roots to Great Britain or Germany.

My grandfather, Clarence Arlington Barnett, was a steelworker and a football player. Grandpa, who was born in Westmoreland County, Pennsylvania in 1880, quit school in eighth grade to go to work in the Waynesburg Steel Mill. Although he never enrolled, Waynesburg College recruited him to play football, a common practice among aggressive small college football programs of that era. Grandpa and three other steelworkers were let off work an hour early to practice with the college boys. The Waynesburg College team, with my grandfather at guard, played a number of other colleges in western Pennsylvania, including what is now the University of Pittsburgh. After the football season Grandpa just worked in the steel mill, but he got to keep the beautiful black sweater with the orange W that he wore to play in the college games.

When he moved to Follansbee he joined the nearby Steubenville Athletic Club's, Big Reds, a semi-professional football team. The

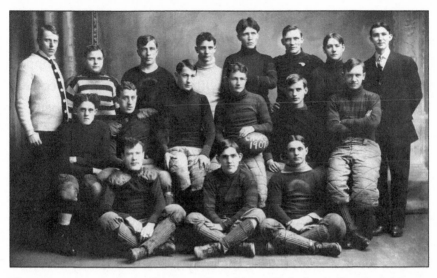

The team picture of the Steubenville Athletic Club football team with my Grandpa Clarence "Fats" Barnett third from the left in row three. Notice the ball proclaiming "Champs 1907.

Big Reds were one of the many semi-pro teams that dotted the Eastern Ohio-Western Pennsylvania region. Grandpa never talked about the team's record, but the team picture, with Grandpa in the back row features a ball proclaiming "Champs 1907."

My grandma, Florence "Flossie" Chariza Marsh was a 1906 graduate of Wellsburg High School (the only one of my grandparents to earn a high school degree). As a high school graduate Flossie was considered to be a refined and well educated young woman. When Clarence and Flossie married in 1908, he was twenty-eight-years-old and she was twenty which was considered old at a time when most people were married in their teens. They set up housekeeping at 954 Neville Street on a steep hillside with a good view of the mill.

Virginia, the first Barnett baby, was born later in 1908. Her birthday was too close to Grandma and Grandpa's wedding date to be respectable so they never celebrated their wedding anniversary. Robert, their only child not to survive into adulthood, was born in

1909 (and died in 1926), and Mary was born in 1913. Then a child came every two years: Paul (1915); Clarence, my dad (1917); Hal (1919); and Hugh (1921). Apparently, as soon as Flossie stopped nursing one, she got pregnant with another. After a three-year break, Doris was born in 1924, Jean in 1927, and Dick, the baby, in 1929. All the Barnett children were born at home; as was the custom for working-class families.

The large Barnett family prospered during the 1920s. Grandpa was a roller, one of the highest paying jobs in the mill. The three oldest children, Virginia, Mary, and Paul all went to college. Then the Great Depression hit the family hard. Grandpa did not work at the mill for two years during the early 1930s. The family survived only because he brought produce home from his brother's farm in Steubenville where he helped out, and the older children worked part-time jobs while they were going to school.

My dad graduated from Follansbee High School in 1935 and attended West Liberty State Teachers College for less than one semester. His sister Mary, who had a teaching job by then, paid his tuition and Dad earned his room and board by working campus jobs that were funded by New Deal programs. But the cold fall weather and the wicked wind that blew across the hilltop campus ended my father's college career. "It was really cold up there on that hill and I didn't have a winter coat," Dad told me later. "I got a job and didn't go back to school after Thanksgiving."

My mom's parents were Robert Wylie Anderson and Hulda Latimer Anderson. Wylie was from Steubenville and Hulda grew up on a farm in the hills back of Follansbee. They set up housekeeping at 616 Banfield Avenue. Bessie their first daughter was born in 1912 at the Ohio Valley General Hospital in Steubenville. My mom, Helen Marie Anderson was born in the same hospital in 1920. As a family rising into the middle class the Andersons believed in having babies born in hospitals.

Grandpa Wylie worked for the streetcar company. He started as a conductor on the route from Steubenville, Ohio to Wheeling, West Virginia but, later was promoted to dispatcher. He worked steadily during the Depression and the Andersons were considered to be well off.

Mom graduated third in the Follansbee High School class of 1937. Although Mom and Dad had dated off and on during high school, in an impulsive moment in the summer of 1937, she married Martin Riehl, the captain of the football team. The impulse quickly wore off and they were divorced in less than a year. Mom later told me she knew pretty quickly that marrying Martin was a mistake; she described him as "dull and boring."

Women rarely asked for divorces in the 1930s, particularly if there was no cruelty or adultery involved. Somehow Mom was able to convince the judge that Martin's being boring was grounds for divorce. The judge granted the divorce, but recognizing an immature and impulsive young woman, he required that she not get married for one year.

Mom and Dad resumed seeing each other soon after the divorce was final, but only in carefully chaperoned situations. Opal Lantz, Mom's "best friend forever" and now more than ninety-years-old, was often the chaperone. "Helen and I would walk down to Jefferson Street and meet your dad. They would talk and maybe kiss a little and then we would walk home," she recalled.

Mom was in a delicate situation as a newly divorced woman with a local boyfriend, but prohibited from marrying for one year. Her family sent her out of town to work for the selective service in Raleigh, North Carolina and Memphis, Tennessee for a year. Dad visited her a couple of times in both places, and they also went on dates on the few occasions when she came back to Follansbee for visits.

At the end of a little more than a year, Mom returned to

Follansbee and she and Dad were married on November 7, 1941. They moved in with Grandma Hulda who had become a widow on the death of Grandpa Wylie in 1938.

Dad was initially rejected from the wartime draft in 1942 because of a suspected heart murmur, but a year later he enlisted and was accepted into the Navy. I was born on March 27, 1943, shortly before my father entered the Navy. During the war I was raised primarily by my mother and grandmother. Mom worked as a teller at the Bank of Follansbee during the war, but resigned from her job as soon as Dad was discharged from the Navy.

I did not have any childhood traumas until March 11, 1949. I had been told for months Mom was going to have a baby and that I would have a new little brother or sister soon. None of that had much impact on me until Mom went to the hospital. Two days later she called me from the hospital to tell me that I had a new baby brother named Jimmy. "Good," I said, "but do you have to bring him home? Can't you leave him in the hospital and we can just visit him there?" When they brought him home against my wishes, I realized I was "off the throne." When Janie came along two years later it didn't make much difference, because by then I was no longer the somewhat spoiled only child. I have to admit that my brother Jimmy and Janie were cute, very good-natured, and fun; traits they carried throughout their lives. It was a little rocky at first, but in a couple of years I came to love them.

Life was good for my parents in Follansbee during the late 1940's. Mom was thin and petite at five-feet even. She had a large bust which when combined with her petite size gave her a stunning figure. With dark red, almost auburn, hair, she was emotional and volatile, much like the stereotypical redhead. Dad was of medium height at five-feet, seven-inches and very thin at less than 135 pounds with dark, wavy hair and brown eyes. He and Mom made

Before Jimmy and Janie when life was good, c. 1944. (Photo by Opal Lantz)

an attractive, young couple. They had a large circle of friends they had know since childhood. Industrial America was at its peak of productivity. There was money to spend on gambling, drinking, and parties, and Mom and Dad enjoyed all of these.

My parents loved Follansbee. They loved to walk down Main Street to the Buffalo Confectionary after dinner for an ice cream cone. On Friday nights they loved going to the Follansbee High School Blue Wave football games, and then getting together with the other Barnetts or going to the American Legion for an after-game drink. On winter evenings they danced to the Tom Care and His Virginians Orchestra at the Venetian Club on Main Street. On summer nights when the smoke from the mill became oppressive, they enjoyed racing in three cars with friends like the Mannings, the Stewarts, the Schwertfegers, the Rogersons, and Opal Lantz and her current boyfriend to the top of Allegheny Street hill and out into the country along Eldersville Road to the Bil-Mar Road House where they could have a few drinks and dance, away from the prying eyes of the townspeople. They reveled in being young and surrounded by familiar places and familiar people.

Like many Appalachians, Mom and Dad had strong ties to their families, almost all of whom stayed in the Follansbee area. Six of my father's eight brothers and sisters lived within a fifteen-minute drive from Neville Street. When Grandma and Grandpa Barnett hosted Sunday dinner, a Christmas celebration, or an after-the-football-game celebration for their children, spouses and grandchildren, it was a raucous affair. Everyone tried to talk at once, people laughed at stories that had been retold a hundred times, and the air was thick with cigarette smoke. It could be an intimidating atmosphere for newcomers used to more sedate family gatherings. Although my mom adapted easily, many of my aunts' and uncles' dates had to go out to the car for a smoke to get away from the confusion. Some never came back, but those who did became such an integral part of the extended family that it became difficult to distinguish between the original Barnetts and the in-laws.

Mom's family was smaller, but equally close. Grandma Anderson stayed on Banfield Avenue after Grandpa Wylie died in 1938. Aunt Norma Gardner lived on Main Street, only a block away, where she owned and operated the James Funeral Home, after her husband's death. Norma was really Mom's second cousin, but they were as close as sisters. Aunt Bess Miller, Uncle Jim, and my cousins

A 1950 photo of the Clarence and Flossie Barnett family in a rare quiet moment. Seated (l to r), Virginia Barnett Burgess, Grandma Flossie Marsh Barnett, Grandpa Clarence A. Barnett, Mary Barnett Gracey; standing (l to r), Jean Barnett Verner, my father Clarence "Nance" Barnett, Dick Barnett, Paul Barnett, Hal Barnett, Hugh Barnett, and Doris Barnett Ficca.

Cindy and Margaret Anne lived in Weirton, only fifteen minutes away. The get-togethers with Mom's side of the family were not as loud as the Barnett's but they were just as much fun and just as loving.

My dad thought that he was smarter than everyone else. He had an excellent memory, knew a lot of facts, and had a good vocabulary. He was an excellent storyteller particularly when he was telling stories about the Barnetts during the Depression or about his Navy career which had consisted mostly of playing poker in Philadelphia and Washington and hitchhiking home to Follansbee. Because he thought he was smarter than everyone else, he believed he could always beat the system by doing things differently than most people. What he did not understand was that in most instances the majority of people make the right decisions in life, because most decisions are easy. Dad was not a logical thinker and tended to over think every decision and outsmart himself. His mantra was, "I do not choose to take the common path."

Not following the common path led Dad into a lot of wrong turns. He figured that if everyone bought one brand the smart choice would be to buy an off brand where he could get a great deal. We spent much of my childhood in search of great deals like the one for my bike. Dad rejected my pleas for a popular Schwinn or Huffy in favor of a Colson—a cheap, flimsy bike with funny handlebars. Dad never figured out that brands were popular for a reason. He outsmarted himself again and again.

Instead of following the common path that led his brother-in-law and six brothers into jobs in the steel industry, Dad decided to sell life insurance. He failed to consider that life insurance is one of the hardest products to sell or that the steel industry was one of the highest paying in the United States. Our relatives were all extremely successful; his family struggled financially.

Dad worked for the Equitable Life Insurance Company, a small company located in the Mid-Atlantic and Midwest. Working out of the Steubenville office Dad was moderately successful at selling small insurance policies to steel workers in Follansbee. He was soon offered a middle management position as staff manager over five other salesmen, and then the position of staff manager over a small satellite office in East Liverpool, Ohio, which was twenty-seven miles and a world away. Dad took the East Liverpool offer and moved us to Newell, believing that he would soon be promoted to manager at a regular office which would offer excellent pay and prestige. This move proved to be another bad choice. Not only was he exiled from his hometown; but sales plummeted for unlike steel workers pottery workers had little discretionary money to spend on the luxury of a life insurance policy. He never received his hoped-for promotion to manager in his thirty-two years with the company.

The smartest decision Dad ever made was to marry Mom, who had much better reasoning abilities and was a harder worker. But Dad almost screwed that up too when he let her marry the captain of the football team.

When we moved to Newell in the spring of 1951 we left a town and a family we loved. We went upriver into new and uncharted waters, where we had no friends and no family. For Appalachians who value place and family, it was a bold move.

Map of West Virginia's Northern Panhandle. (Map created by Jim Atkinson)

A pile of dishes at the Newell dump ready to be pushed over the edge by a bulldozer. (1992 photo taken by Michael Keller courtesy of *Goldenseal Magazine*)

Chapter 2

The World's Greatest Dump

Newell was at its peak when we arrived there in 1951. The population had reached an all-time high of 2,101. The Homer Laughlin China Company, the largest pottery in the world, was the epicenter of the American pottery industry, and both the Globe Brick Company and the Edwin M. Knowles China Company were working full steam. The basketball team had advanced through the Class "B" state basketball tournament all the way to the area tournament. Fortunately, they had most of the same team returning for the 1951 - 52 season. Both Jefferson Elementary School, a state of the art school, and Waterford Park, a one-mile thoroughbred horserace track located two and one-half-miles south of Newell, were set to open that year.

Don't get the idea that Newell was one of those picturesque villages with green lawns and white picket fences. It wasn't like that in the fifties and never had been. The streets were tar and gravel and filled with potholes, winter and summer. Most of the town did not have sidewalks. We walked on dirt paths with plenty of mud puddles. Newell was an unincorporated pottery town dominated by The Homer Laughlin China Company. The pottery industry was

The remains of the old Newell Park fountain in 1992 (Photo by Michael Keller courtesy of *Goldenseal Magazine*)

notoriously low paying and used a large number of unskilled and semiskilled workers. Even though Homer Laughlin was an industry leader in both ceramic technology and china designs, it was never a high-profit or high-wage industry like the steel mill and potteries were soon to face serious competition from foreign imports.

But we kids thought we lived in the greatest town in the world. We felt sorry for the children who had to grow up in cities like New York, Pittsburgh, and even Weirton or Follansbee. We had woods, fields, two nice playgrounds, and our most treasured resource—the town dump.

Most towns hid their dumps in some out-of-the-way place, but not Newell. We were proud of our dump, which was located on the main drag, Washington Street. In fact, the dump was located across the street from Newell High School and the football and baseball fields.

The contents of the dump were not the run-of-the-mill type garbage, but refuse unique to Newell. The Homer Laughlin China Company used the valley to discard the waste products from the pottery production. The dump was not offensive. It didn't smell except for the acrid smoke from an occasional fire. (We did not know about toxic waste then.) Actually, the long, white wall of dishes that cascaded into the valley was kind of pretty and would have been considered a wonder had it been located somewhere else, say Dover, England.

Beauty aside, the dump was wonderful for the endless number of recreational activities it could sustain, ranging from mountain climbing, art and big game hunting to dish breaking and plate sailing. It was truly a multipurpose, multigenerational facility, though in the 1950s these terms had yet to enter the lexicon. Thousands of dishes, saucers, platters, cups, and pitchers of all sizes and shapes stood in piles about four or five feet tall waiting to be pushed over the edge by a bulldozer. These pieces of ware were rejected at various stages of production. Some pieces were completely decorated and glazed, with flaws so slight they were almost impossible to find. Most pieces, however, had been cracked when they were fired, so they were unglazed, raw, white, and rough to the touch.

The dump was begun sometime around 1907 when The Homer Laughlin China Company opened in Newell and began to dump rejected dishes, molds, clay, dyes, and other stuff used to make pottery in a narrow valley just past Sixth Street. In their first years of operation, they dumped enough waste to build a road along the Ohio River connecting the two sections of their plant. Later, they filled in enough of the valley to build a road across its middle, now Washington Street and West Virginia State Route 2. When these roads were completed, the pottery began to create a wall of dishes along the south side of the valley between the two new roads.

⌒

I first encountered the dump shortly after my family moved to Newell. My ten-year-old cousin, Bob Gracey, and I were sent outside to play while Mom and Aunt Mary unpacked the kitchen. The day was chilly and grey and no other kids were anywhere to be found. We walked to the playground and then to the baseball field, which were less than a block from our new home, and both seemed pretty ordinary. But off in the distance loomed something we had never seen before, and we were drawn to it like proverbial moths to a flame.

There it was—a virtual wall of dishes more than an eighth of a mile long and going down about thirty-five or forty feet to the green valley below. We had discovered the Newell dump, a place of wonder and adventure. We later learned the dump was called "the fill" because the waste from the pottery was used to fill up the narrow valley that ran through the middle of Newell. We quickly discovered the first fill activity, mountain climbing. Sure, we threw some dishes and broke some cups, but we were in the mood to explore. The wall of dishes was steep but not vertical, and climbing down looked easy. However, we soon discovered the broken dishes were slippery and a wrong step could cause an avalanche. The rough and sharp, unglazed dishes hurt our hands and tore our pants. From the floor of the valley, the wall of dishes looked awesome. Dark and bubbling liquids oozed from steel drums. We had to knock over only one to learn never to do it again.

When we got home, we discovered clay had stuck to every conceivable part of our shoes and even to one of my socks. A flour-like white substance clung to our jackets, and our pants were torn and bloody. We argued we were not dirty in the technical sense of having brown or black dirt on us, but Mom and Aunt Mary seemed unable to grasp our fine point of logic and two solid, old-fashioned spankings followed.

Despite threats and punishments, we returned to the dump year after year, taking part in the full range of activities, including collecting. Anyone who has ever been to a dump knows the urge to collect, the desire to take home other people's junk, and even to bring home some of your own. Once you see it laying out at the dump, you cannot bear to part with it.

At the dump, the collectibles were dishes, and my little sister Janie became a master collector. Often, she found only slightly cracked, fully glazed and decorated dishes and cups that she would bring home and proudly present to Mom as gifts. Her prize possession was the full set of unglazed dinnerware she brought home and decorated with crayons. She had to be one of the few girls anywhere to have her own full set of adult-size dishes with a lot of pink and blue designs to use for her dolls' tea parties. Most of the cups had handles, and all had cracks.

Big game hunting, not my cup of tea, was nevertheless one of the more popular fill activities. On warm evenings, more than ten or fifteen cars parked on the river end of the fill and the sound of .22 caliber rifle fire was fairly constant. During twilight the hunters stood on the top rim of the dishes and shot rats as they came out on the pottery below. After dark, however, they taped flashlights on the gunstocks to "freeze" their prey before shooting.

During my high school years in the late 1950s, I discovered the therapeutic value of the most popular dump activity, dish breaking and sailing. Teenagers in many towns brooded in their rooms, but in Newell we went to the dump. After an hour or so of breaking and sailing dishes, our problems did not seem as fierce. We broke dishes by slamming them on the ground, throwing them against each other, or by sticking them upright in soft clay and then throwing cups or dishes at them, shooting-gallery style. That was just crude destruction, but felt so good.

Sailing dishes demanded more skill. Basically, a dish turned upside down and thrown out over the edge of the fill sailed somewhat like a modern-day Frisbee. Because the dishes were heavier and less aerodynamic than Frisbees, they could not be thrown backhanded, Frisbee style, but required a baseball pitcher's sidearm throw. Glazed dishes were a little slippery to throw. The rough, unglazed ones provided a better grip but eventually left blisters on your hand. The oblong meat platters looked funniest as they flew over the edge of the fill, but were so heavy some of them took two hands to maneuver. No little dog would ever try to catch one of those platters in his mouth. Dinner plates were good; too heavy to travel far, they usually crashed satisfyingly into the side of the wall of dishes. Salad plates and saucers were the best to throw. Under the right conditions they would sail out over the wall of dishes, catch some rising air current, miss the trees in the valley below, and almost reach the creek forty yards away. Bad throws, those that tipped one way or the other, would dive like demented kamikazes into the wall of dishes.

The greatest feat of dish sailing was performed by a high school kid a couple years older than I was. Denny Wells once sailed a butter plate more than eighty yards across the dump into the hill on the other side. Actually, Denny was a fine high school athlete, but in the spring of his junior year he quit the baseball team to spend more time at the dump. We watched him throw beautiful "sailers" over the edge of the dump hour after hour, often well into the twilight. Later, we found out why he was spending so much time at the fill. After the end of the school year, we heard he and his girlfriend had eloped and he had joined the Marines.

When I was grown up with my own family and visiting my mother-in-law, Alma Witherow, in Chester, I would sometimes take our daughters to the dump. "You're going to take the girls where?"

Grandmother Alma asked disapprovingly the first time. But she changed her tune when the girls gave her a gift of a cup and saucer they had decorated themselves.

Then there was that beautiful late summer day in 1989 when my brother, sister, and I and our families were going to the Barnett family reunion in Follansbee. The morning of the reunion we loaded up two cars with our kids, including our daughters Megan (17) and Alexis (13); Janie's daughter, Katie (4); and Jim's sons, Beau (4) and Alex (2-1/2), and headed to Newell and the dump. Everything was exactly the same, or so it seemed to us. And with a little prodding, our children of the video game age took up the ancient sports of breaking, sailing, and climbing. Perhaps all hope is not lost for today's kids. If placed in the right environment, they

Carrying on a family tradition, the Barnetts and Powells at the dump in 1989. From left to right are Larry Powell, Katie Powell, Jane Barnett Powell, the author, and Alexis Barnett.

can make their own fun just as we did many years ago. It is a shame none of us lives in a town with a good dump.

As we walked back to the cars after a solid hour of fun, we were covered with white dust. Beau's tennis shoe, sucked off in wet clay, was filthy but at least back on his foot. Janie, looked over to me and asked, "Do you think Mom and Dad will like these matching cups? You can hardly see the cracks."

Chapter 3

The Home of the Largest Pottery in the World

When I moved to Newell in 1951, I felt like a displaced person. The town was about twenty-six miles north of our home in Follansbee. As an adult who has not lived there for more than forty years, I am tempted to say it was only about twenty-six miles north, but I would never have said "only twenty-six miles" as a child or as a resident of either Follansbee or Newell. To us, twenty-six miles was a journey and our identity was firmly rooted in the place where we lived. Although the towns, both small, industrialized communities clinging to wide spots in the Ohio Valley, may have seemed similar to outsiders, to us the difference was stark; only one of them was home. In fact, I found living in Newell so disorienting that during the year after our move, I would frequently get up from my seat in the second grade classroom and run to the windows to look out and try to determine where I was.

Of course, my first day at the new school had been traumatic and may have contributed to my need to orient myself. My mom put me on the city bus from East Liverpool for the six-block ride to school. She told me I was to come home on the bus, which made a run through Newell every thirty minutes. The other kids from the lower end of Newell who were waiting for the bus promised to help me get on the right bus after school. Unfortunately, I was so excited after school that I ran ahead of the other kids from the lower end and was separated from them when I reached the crosswalk half a block from school. Confused, I asked the patrol boy where the stop for the East Liverpool bus was. Why East Liverpool? The name just popped into my head; my dad worked there and my parents had talked about moving there for weeks before they found a house in Newell. The patrol boy pointed to a bus stop across Fourth Street. It looked fine to me because it was where I had gotten off the bus that morning. The bus came right away and I immediately got on, standing by the coin box waiting for my stop. I was surprised that none of the other kids got on the bus, but thought I was lucky to catch it because I had run so fast. It seemed to be taking a lot longer to get home than it had to get to school that morning. Then the bus headed out of Newell. I knew I was going in the wrong direction. But it wasn't until the bus headed over the bridge and across the Ohio River that I was terrified enough to speak to the driver.

"Where is this bus going?" I asked the driver. "East Liverpool," he replied. "But I live in Newell," I said with a catch in my voice. He looked me up and down and saw a very small second grade boy on the verge of tears. His voice softened and he said, "Stay on this bus and I'll take you home when I make the next run." "But I don't have any money or a bus ticket," I said. "Don't worry," he said with a huge smile. "If you don't get off the bus you don't have to pay again." He got off the bus when we pulled into the East Liverpool bus terminal and said, "Wait here; I'll leave again in fifteen minutes." I spent those fifteen minutes, which seemed like hours, holding on to the coin box as the bus sat in the terminal.

True to his word, the driver came out fifteen minutes later and drove to Newell. After we passed the elementary school bus stop, things began to look familiar. I knew I was close to home when I saw the dump and the baseball field. As the bus turned the corner onto Grant Street, I shouted, "There is my house!" and took one hand off the coin box to point, but replaced it quickly.

As the bus came to a stop, I released my death grip on the coin box and bounded for the door even before it was open. Mom gave me a big hug as I raced through the front door, and said, "I was worried when you didn't get off the bus with the other kids and was just about to bundle Jimmy up and come looking for you. I'm glad you're home." I was glad too.

Once it became home, I was always glad to see the "Newell Unincorporated" signs that sat at each end of town. Since it was unincorporated, Newell did not have a city government, so we received all our services from the Hancock County government, which meant no police protection, streets with massive potholes, and few sidewalks. There weren't even any traffic lights in town when I moved there, although Newell did get a traffic light the next

The sign says it all.

Aerial picture of Newell looking from north to south taken in 1957. (Photo from the 1957 Newell High School Yearbook)

year when the Waterford Park racetrack opened just down the road from town. The new red light, blinking yellow twenty hours a day, was a reminder of how little traffic passed by; but for most of us, it was a beacon of progress and source of pride—a real traffic light right here in Newell, West Virginia.

It wasn't surprising that a red light was needed four hours a day for the twin traffic juggernauts of racetrack traffic and pottery shift changes. We were a pottery town where almost everyone worked at The Homer Laughlin China Company or just down the block at the Edwin M. Knowles China Company. Before the red light, cars were often backed up for the entire two blocks from the plants' parking lots to Washington Street.

Since almost everyone worked for a pottery, and the pottery industry was notoriously low paying and labor intensive, the town was almost completely working class or working poor, and dominated by a blue-collar mentality. Newell was a blend of Appalachian fatalism, immigrants' optimism, blue-collar values, and the 1950s dream of the materialistic good life in America.

⸺

Newell is located on the Ohio River in the foothills of the Appalachian Mountains at the very top of West Virginia's Northern Panhandle—close to the point where the states of West Virginia, Ohio, and Pennsylvania meet. We placed ourselves by our proximity to our great rival, Chester, one mile northeast of us, and to our metropolitan neighbor, East Liverpool, Ohio a town of about 20,000 situated just across the Ohio River. Outsiders who came to the racetrack were more likely to think of us as being thirty-seven miles northwest of Pittsburgh, Pennsylvania.

At its core, Newell is clearly a product of geology and geography. Newell is in the Appalachian Mountains which were formed between 30 and 65 million years ago when a series of continental plate compressions pushed flat-lying strata east to west in a series of uplifted folds. Another 50 million years of weathering and erosion left the Appalachian Mountains basically as we see them today except for the changes brought about by the Ice Age.[1]

West Virginia lies just south of the reach of the Ice Age glaciers, but as the glaciers retreated, massive amounts of water were released when the ice began to melt and formed large lakes trapped by ice dams. When the dams broke up, erosion from the huge rivers of water that spilled forth helped carve the steep bluffs and shelves that form the course of many of the modern rivers in Appalachia, including the Ohio River and the Ohio River Valley. Present-day Newell sits on one of the ledges from the ancient riverbed created by the melting Ice Age glaciers.[2]

That narrow ledge slopes gently from a set of tall hills down to the banks of the Ohio River. The ledge is about a mile long running from a series of cliffs close to the riverbank at its northern end and spreading to about a quarter of a mile at its widest point. When I arrived in the 1950s, all the available land for housing had been built on. There was no opportunity for the population to increase because all of the land was in use for either industry or housing. Only ten blocks long and five blocks wide, Newell was defined by the space between hill and river.

We were taught nothing about the early history of Newell in either American or West Virginia history classes. Perhaps that was for the best because the earliest settlers in Newell were murderers and warmongers. In 1770 Daniel Greathouse, an Indian scout, settled his family in what is now Newell and built a blockhouse for protection from Native Americans. In April 1774, Greathouse, Samuel Muchmore, and a couple other settlers enticed seven Native Americans (five men, a woman, and a child) who were camped south of Newell on the opposite side of the Ohio River near Yellow Creek, to cross the river. The settlers gave the Native Americans rum until three of them were so drunk they passed out. The settlers engaged the other two in a shooting contest and after the Native Americans emptied their guns, the settlers shot them dead. They shot the woman when she attempted to run, and then cruelly butchered the three sleeping Native Americans with a tomahawk. The baby was spared because the mother had convinced the whites it was the baby of a white man.

This unprovoked and unspeakably cruel murder of the Native Americans became known as Logan's Massacre, because three of the murdered Native Americans were the father, brother, and sister of Logan, the great chief of the Mingo tribe, who had heretofore been a strong advocate of peace with the white settlers. The murders started Lord Dunmore's War and ten years of brutal warfare that cost the lives of more than forty settlers and as many Native Americans.[3]

We were also never taught why Newell was stuck on the very far reaches of the northern panhandle of West Virginia, far removed from the rest of the state instead of being in either Ohio or Pennsylvania the major parts of both of which seemed much closer. Newell is in West Virginia only because of a very arbitrary quirk of surveying and, of course, the Civil War. In 1779, Charles Mason and Jeremiah Dixon surveyed the border between Maryland, Virginia, and Pennsylvania for a distance of 233 miles stopping in what is now Monongalia County, West Virginia. The boundary, which became known as the Mason-Dixon Line, was subsequently extended in 1795 by David Rittenhouse and Andrew Endicott to complete the southern border of Pennsylvania. Rittenhouse and Endicott stopped twenty-five miles short of the Ohio River because Pennsylvania wanted a square southwest corner. Consequently, the north-south boundary of the state was drawn at a ninety-degree angle to the Mason-Dixon Line at a point where the boundary would cross the survey stone marking the edge of the Northwest Territory and would give Pennsylvania its square corner and a straight

Map of West Virginia with the Mason-Dixon Line. (Map created by Jim Atkinson)

western border running from the Mason-Dixon line to Lake Erie. This left a sliver of land extending northward like a spear thrust up between the border of Pennsylvania and the Ohio River. On the tip of that sliver, the northern panhandle of Virginia, sat the future site of Newell. If the Northwest Territory marker had been ten miles to the west, Newell would have been part of Pennsylvania; or if the river had been ten miles to the east, Newell would have been in Ohio.[4]

The name Newell first appeared in 1837 when John Newell from Fairview, Virginia bought part of the Greathouse land. Mr. Newell laid out lots on the land that he wasn't farming and a

29

small community grew up.[5] Of course when Virginia seceded from the Union in 1861 West Virginia promptly seceded from Virginia completing the process of becoming a state in 1863.

⁓

The first major industry to locate in the Newell area was the Globe Brick Company. In the 1890s John Porter, a businessman from nearby New Cumberland, West Virginia purchased twenty-five acres just south of Newell, because the area was rich in clay. Porter built the Globe Brick Company to make street paving bricks, but when brick streets gave way to asphalt and cement streets Globe Brick began to make the bricks that were used to line the steel ladles of Carnegie Steel in Pittsburgh and of Weirton Steel located nineteen miles to the south in Weirton, West Virginia. As the steel industry prospered, so did Globe Brick.[6]

However, the driving force behind the development of Newell was The Homer Laughlin China Company, which opened its Newell plant in 1907. The firm was already a thriving concern before it moved to Newell. The company, originally known as the Laughlin Brothers Pottery, had been founded in 1873 by two brothers, Homer and Shakespeare Laughlin, who came from a family that must have known and loved good literature to name their sons after famous authors. At that time the city council of East Liverpool, Ohio offered a prize of $5,000 to anyone who would build a four-kiln pottery devoted to manufacturing white china. East Liverpool was a pottery center but the local potteries produced a yellow ware that could not compete with the harder, lighter white china that was imported from England. The Laughlin brothers were able to produce the white ware and won the prize even though the pottery they built had only two bottle kilns.

Bottle kilns were the industry standard for producing pottery from the 1870s to the 1920s. The kilns were brick structures resembling giant wine bottles forty feet or more in height. Ware was placed inside the hollow kiln, the opening was bricked up and the kiln was heated by coal or wood fires around openings along the bottom. After the ware was heated long enough to be fired, the kiln was then allowed to cool. When the kiln was cool enough, the potters removed the finished ware from the kiln.

The Laughlin brothers soon began to produce semi-porcelain, white china that was as good, if not better, than china produced in England. Moreover, the Laughlin china could be sold at a price that middle-class Americans could afford. The company was a success. To symbolize its ascendance, the company developed a logo which it stamped on the back of each dish showing a large cursive "L" surrounding an American eagle on top of the English lion that it had subdued.[7]

Despite the company's success, the Laughlin brothers soon became bored with pottery. Shakespeare sold his share of the business to Homer in 1877. It was not long until Homer also tired of running the plant and began to spend less time there. Fortunately, he had hired a local man, W.E. Wells, from Brooke County, West Virginia as a bookkeeper in 1889. Wells, proved to be an able assistant, and rose to the position of general manager while in his twenties. When Homer began to take extended trips, which happened with increasing frequency, Wells was left in charge.[8]

In 1897, Laughlin approached Wells with an opportunity to buy the plant. Wells' great-grandson, Joseph Wells III, the current president of Homer Laughlin, recently described the meeting: "Laughlin said something to the effect of 'I'm tired of playing in the mud. I want to do something else and you are the only one here who has the moxie to run this place. I want you to buy it.' Well, my great-grandfather didn't have two nickels to rub together at that point. So he hooked up with the Aaron family in Pittsburgh. I am not sure exactly how it happened, but I think that the Aarons were venture capitalists."[9]

Louis I. Aaron did have money to invest. He had been born in the Prussian region of Germany in 1840 and in 1857 immigrated to the United States, where he lived in New York and Atlanta before settling in Pittsburgh, Pennsylvania. There he made his money in the brewing industry. On December 7, 1897, Wells and the Aaron family officially purchased The Homer Laughlin China Company and began a business relationship that would last for four generations. "The Aarons were the majority stockholders and financial advisers, but they charged the Wells family with running the business," said Joseph Wells III.[10]

With Wells as the secretary-treasurer and general manager and Aaron as president and majority stockholder, the company prospered. Most of their sales were to the F.W. Woolworth Company, a rapidly expanding thrift chain, and to the American Cereal Company, which packed Homer Laughlin cereal bowls in boxes of Mother's Oats. The Homer Laughlin operation quickly expanded and built two new plants in East Liverpool. Soon growing demand for their dishes made additional expansion necessary. There was no land available for industrial development in East Liverpool, however.

Aaron and Wells realized if they wanted to grow they would need to find a new location. Across the Ohio River, there was a strip of flat land a mile long and a quarter mile wide at the site of the Newell farm. In September 1902 Wells, the Aarons, and a number of other East Liverpool pottery owners bought 428 acres, in what is now Newell, for $75,000. In November, they formed the North American Manufacturing Company, capitalized at $1 million, to develop industrial sites in Newell. The North American Manufacturing Company formed the Newell Bridge Company, the Newell Street Railway Company, the Newell Power and Water Company, the Newell Lake Park Company, and the Lake Newell Floral Company.[11]

Building a bridge across the Ohio River so that workers and materials could easily reach Newell from East Liverpool was the first order of business. On June 2, 1904 work began to build a suspension bridge from a bluff on the west end of East Liverpool to a very narrow shelf of land carved out of the hill on the West Virginia side of the river. The 1600-foot-long suspension bridge was completed a year later. On July 4, 1905, the Newell Bridge was officially opened when W.E. Wells and Edwin M. Knowles drove across the bridge in Knowles' 1904 Pope automobile. Manufactured by the Pope Car Company of Toledo, Ohio this automobile was one of fewer than

Edwin M. Knowles is shown in his 1904 Pope automobile that was the first automobile to cross the Newell Bridge when it was completed on July 4, 1905. W.E. Wells was a passenger in the car followed by 1,000 people on foot. (Photo owned by the East Liverpool Historical Society, provided courtesy of the Museum of Ceramics, East Liverpool, Ohio)

a dozen automobiles in East Liverpool. A crowd of almost 1,000 people walked across the bridge following the automobile.[12]

The Newell streetcar line, which ran from East Liverpool across the bridge, through Newell, and circled what was to become Newell Park, began operating ten days later. Work began immediately on The Homer Laughlin China Company factory in Newell. Not only workers but sightseers also rode the streetcar from East Liverpool to Newell to watch the construction and to picnic in the cleared areas of Laurel Hollow.

The new factory, completed in 1907, was by far the biggest pottery in the world and made Homer Laughlin the world leader in the manufacture of pottery. The six-story factory was 664 feet by 450 feet with 30 bottle kilns, and employed 1,200 workers. Wells, the general manager, was the face of Homer Laughlin, and most people in the area, not surprisingly, believed that the Wells family was the sole owner of the pottery and associated businesses.

Wells was from a Northern Panhandle family with deep roots

Newell Street Railroad pre 1920. (Photo courtesy of the Hancock County Historical Museum)

in the region dating back to 1776. He had graduated from high school in nearby Steubenville and was married to a local woman, Elizabeth Mahan from Follansbee. In 1907, the Wells family built a thirteen-room mansion in the hill top overlooking the developing town and pottery. Described as stately and tasteful, the three-story, white stone house, flanked by a portico and colonial style columns supporting its two-story porch, was a fitting residence for an industrial baron. The Wells family lived in Newell, were active in the community, sent their children to school there, and four generations of the family have managed the firm.

In fact, Wells and Aaron continued the division of responsibility established when they purchased Homer Laughlin in 1897 with Wells as general manager and Aaron as president. Aaron was simply not as visible to those outside the company. He continued to live in Pittsburgh where he could fully participate in the religious and cultural life of the Jewish community. He was a leader in local and regional Jewish communal organizations, and a trustee in the Congregation Rodef Shalom in Pittsburgh.[13] However, he continued to take an active role in managing the company and commuted daily from Pittsburgh to Newell, a drive of more than an hour.

The Wells and Aaron families continued an amicable business relationship in managing Homer Laughlin through four generations. "The Aarons were involved in the business and were involved up until the last day, basically as financial advisers. I've got to say this, the relationship between the Aaron family and the Wells family was an unbelievably good relationship. We never had a vote at a board meeting, never. We always came to an agreement. That was how the trust was between the two families. An Aaron always had the general title of president. Their office was right next door to this office. In the early years they were always in the office," said Joseph Wells III.[14]

Under the leadership of Wells and Aaron, demand for Homer

Laughlin dishes continued to grow and the company continued to expand. The company added a sixteen-kiln plant which its brochure described as "one-story, well-ventilated and scientifically illuminated; a marvel of construction in matters of convenience, comfort and sanitation." "Newell represents," the brochure proclaimed, "the greatest pottery manufacturing project ever carried out."[15] Hyperbole aside, by the 1920s Homer Laughlin had seventy-eight kilns which produced two and a half times more than the second largest pottery. One-tenth of all of the pottery produced in the nation came from Homer Laughlin in Newell, West Virginia.[16]

Homer Laughlin had followed the lead of other major industries by investing capital to create large factories with machine technology that could produce goods efficiently and increase profits through economies of scale. Standard Oil and Carnegie Steel were early leaders in this process, and were quickly followed during the first quarter of the twentieth century by McCormick Harvester, Remington Typewriters, Dow Chemicals, Heinz Foods, and Ford Motor Company. The pottery industry had been resistant to this pattern because it was labor-intensive and required numerous steps in the production process, but Aaron and Wells believed that the same principles that applied to making steel, automobiles, or catsup could apply to making dishes. Building the Newell plants had been the first step in the process. Although they increased the size and mechanization of their operation, the plant, like the pottery industry as a whole, remained a labor-intensive industry. However, the jobs changed from being skilled trades to becoming increasingly semiskilled or assembly-line labor.

In addition to the bridge and trolley companies, the North American Manufacturing Company started the Newell Park. The park was to be a destination at the end of the Newell trolley line that would be attractive enough to encourage people to ride the trolley on the weekends. The man responsible for creating the park was George Washington Clarke (sometimes spelled Clark), Homer Laughlin's vice-president for sales, and a legend as a salesman in the pottery industry in the early 1900s. "He had a strong interest in recreation," said Joseph Wells III. "I think he talked [the] Homer Laughlin [company] into putting a lot of money into the park."[17]

The park was located in Laurel Hollow, a deep valley created by the Sixth Street Hill Creek, which bisected Newell at almost the center of town. The creek was dammed to form a small lake big enough for rowboats at the end of the park nearest the river. Paths bordered by flowers and picnic grounds ran through the valley. Postcards from the era show a seal pen, a monkey cage, a coon pit, beautiful flower beds and floral clock, and a bear cave. The park had a spectacular opening in 1906 and during its first year in operation, motion pictures such as *A Foreigner's Mustache, The Butcher's Nightmare,* and *Dr. Dippy's Sanitarium* were shown at night

Postcard view of the fountain at the Newell Park taken 1909. (Courtesy of Fred and Colleen Waggle, the Tri-State Genealogical & Historical Society)

in a small outdoor theatre. The following year the theatre hosted violinists and amateur talent contests.

In its heyday the Newell Park's zoo had exotic animals like monkeys, seals, and polar bears in addition to more commonplace animals such as burros, deer, geese, and raccoons.[18] However, the skills of Clarke may not have been adequate for managing a zoo. Clarke purchased a female polar bear from the New York Zoological Society and installed her in the bear cave with its entrance blocked. A male polar bear arrived the following day from an animal importer in New York. Clarke had the male bear confined to the cage in front of the cave. Although zoologists had warned against it, Clarke had the cave opened on May 23, 1909, after the bears had been in residence for a day. The female bear immediately attacked the male bear, which responded by knocking the female down and biting her. The animals fought to the death in front of a large crowd of picnickers who were joined by more than 3,000 curiosity seekers who flocked to the park from Newell and East Liverpool.[19] In a rare picture that was taken shortly after the fight, the badly wounded, larger bear is shown standing over his dead victim.[20] A taxidermist, hired quickly to preserve the remains of the dead bear, discovered that the female was actually a male bear. Two male bears in the same cage often led to a fight.

Despite its early success, the park closed after 1914, the year following Clarke's death. "George Washington Clarke died in 1913 and there wasn't anybody at Homer Laughlin who had the interest to run the park, so it just went downhill," said Joseph Wells III.[21] Although the park was officially closed, it became the unofficial playground for generations of Newell boys. Soon after I moved to Newell in 1951, I was taken down the hill past the dump to the floor of the valley and shown the ruins of the old park, not unlike a guest being shown ancient ruins by archaeologists.

Later, my best friend, Larry Hutton, and I spent our elementary school years exploring the park and contemplating what seemed to us to be something built by an earlier civilization. A wall of dishes was beginning to creep out from the dump over what had been the lake, but the remains of the monkey house and seal pit were still clearly visible. The iron cages had been removed for scrap during World War I but the stone foundation of the monkey house was there, about sixty feet by sixty feet, and we could imagine it topped by a cage and filled with monkeys. The seal pit was almost fully intact. In the center was a round, stone platform about thirty feet in diameter and four feet high. Around the platform was what must have been a moat three or four feet deep, eight or ten feet across with a wall six feet high on the outside. We used the seal pit as a fort for various games ranging from cowboys to World War II. We also liked to sit on our knees, slap our hands together, and give a hoarse "arf," to beg for fish.

By the time I visited the park, Washington Street and State Route 2 had been built across the park grounds, and a large tunnel under the road provided a path for the creek and for little boys who were brave enough to stomp through it. The upper half of the valley contained the bear cave and the stone outline of what we thought was a pony ring, but really had been the fountain. The fountain was only a circular natural stone ring, but the bear cave was more interesting. The cave was dug back into the hill with an inside room made from natural stones cemented together over a dirt floor. The inside room was about fifteen feet by twenty-five feet with a hole in the top so food could be dropped into the cage to the bears. The natural stone front wall of the cave was about fifteen feet high and forty feet long and a pit for the bears to swim in could still be seen in front of the cave. It seemed a magical and exotic place that sparked our curiosity and imaginations just as it did for generations of other children who grew up in Newell.

———

Although the park was short-lived, the town of Newell continued to grow. By 1907 the Edwin M. Knowles China Company had opened a fifteen-kiln factory next door to the Homer Laughlin plant. While many of the potters continued to live in East Liverpool and ride the trolley to work in Newell, a growing number of workers chose to live in Newell and walk to work. A post office was established in 1906, and by 1908 Newell had 150 houses and a population of about 576 residents.

The Homer Laughlin and Knowles factories created a huge demand for workers in Newell in the early 1900s. The North American Manufacturing Company advertised widely for potters to come to the East Liverpool, Chester, Newell, and Wellsville area. The ads claimed that the new potteries would need one thousand new men and extolled the advantages of working there. "Colossal industries...and manifold advantages...a place where natures advantages have been perfected by the ingenuity of man guided by the most modern methods," read one pamphlet.[22]

The advertisements drew workers to Newell; many came from the farms of Appalachian Ohio and West Virginia because of the prospect of a factory job and a steady paycheck. Walter and Nancy Nease, the grandparents of my friends Mary and Carol Nease, came from New Haven, West Virginia in Mason County 150 miles to the south of Newell so that Walter could work in the pottery. Walter later ran the Newell Water Company. Their three children graduated from Newell High School when it was located in the Fourth Street School building. Their twin sons Clarence (who was Mary and Carol's father) and Lawrence played on the 1922 Newell High School football team.[23]

Larry Hutton's maternal grandparents, Cecil and Oleta Phillips (although everyone called her Do Do because that what Larry called her when he was too young to say grandma), came from a rural area near Pennsboro, West Virginia, a small town in the northwestern highlands of West Virginia, so that Cecil could work in the pottery. He worked there until the day he died in 1954.[24]

However, the growing industries in the Newell area could not recruit enough American labor. Captain John Porter, the founder of the Globe Brick Company, so desperately needed clay miners that he traveled to Poland to personally recruit Polish miners to come to the United States. "My grandfather Frank Gibas and his two brothers Joe and Walter were recruited by Captain Porter, around the beginning of the century," said Marilyn Gibas. "Porter paid their passage from Poland to come to Newell to work in the clay mines. Joe and Walter made some money and went back to Poland, but my grandfather liked it here and stayed. My dad later was a bricklayer for Globe Brick."[25] A number of other Polish families like the Juszczak, Derda, and Franczek families, who lived in the lower end section of Newell, had fathers or grandfathers who immigrated from Poland and decided to stay.

The North American Manufacturing Company also followed the pattern of other large manufacturing companies and began to advertise for workers among the new immigrants coming into Ellis Island in New York and even in foreign countries. "Why live in a dark hampered stuffy noisy street when you can locate in a blithesome cheerful sunny spot...?" asked one overblown advertisement. The ad then described Newell in glowing terms as the answer. "Newell affords fresh air, pure filtered water...an ideal home...," the ad stated. It concluded with, "In your wildest stretch of the imagination you cannot conceive of a more beautiful spot.... You have never had presented to you such an unexpected opportunity,"[26]

The largest number of foreign-born workers in Newell came from Italy, as part of the great immigration of Italians to the United States in the 1890s and early 1900s. The Laneves, the largest family in Newell, were the best example of how Italian immigrants were recruited to Newell.

The Laneve family originally lived in the Region of Calabria in the rural Province of Cosenza in the most southern part of Italy. Cosenza forms the foot of the boot shaped peninsula, close to the island of Sicily. Because of the difficulty of making a living in its rugged terrain and the lawlessness of the Italian mafia in Calabria, the Laneves decided to immigrate to the United States in the early 1900s. The two oldest sisters and the oldest brother traveled to the United States in 1904 and worked in New York. The three sent money back to Italy to pay for the passage of their six brothers and the parents to come to the new country. The process took almost ten years. During that time the family decided when everyone was in the United States they would migrate to Newell, West Virginia. They had been attracted by the advertisements posted around the Ellis Island terminal describing the wonders of living and working in Newell. When the youngest children, Ralph and Carmen, arrived with their parents, the older siblings told them of their decision to move to Newell to take jobs that had been promised to all of them.

The family traveled by train to Newell in 1914 and was very pleased with the rural, hilly terrain that reminded them of their native Calabria. On their arrival, the seven brothers were hired to work at Homer Laughlin and worked there the rest of their lives.[27]

All the brothers stayed in Newell to raise their families. In 1924, Ralph, then twenty-six years old, married Rose DeStefano, the sixteen-year-old daughter of a grocery store owner from Monessen, Pennsylvania whose family was also Calabrese. Ralph brought his new bride back to Newell, where they raised a family of fourteen children (nine boys and five girls). The other seven Laneve brothers followed the same pattern, and by the time they had raised their families in the 1950s, there were more than fifty Laneves living in Newell or about 2.5% of the population of the town.[28]

For some unknown reason, probably a mistake at the Ellis Island immigration desk, the last name of brothers Sam and Carmen had only one capital letter, Laneve. The last name of the rest of the

Five of the seven Laneve/LaNeve brothers, originally from Italy, immigrated to America ending their migration in Newell, West Virginia. (Photo from *The History of Newell and Vicinity*, reprinted by The Tri-State Genealogical & Historical Society, 1995)

family was spelled with a capital N, LaNeve. Despite being cousins Ron and John spelled their names differently. "During our school days, friends kidded the LaNeve children that they were the "fancy people," said Ron.

All the boys were excellent athletes and especially good basketball players. There was not a Newell high school basketball team in the period from 1945 through 1956 without a Laneve or LaNeve on the team. The 1951 - 52 championship team had Ron and John on the starting team and Paul on the roster.

Like many immigrant families, the Laneves strongly encouraged their children to become educated. "My father and his brothers did not speak very good English, but my father was educated because he read every newspaper he could get his hands on," said Joan LaNeve Martin. "He would not speak Italian to us kids because he said, 'We are in America and we need to speak American.'"[29]

The Laneve family was very successful in educating the first generation born in America so that they could enter a profession. Five of the Laneve cousins became teachers (three taught me in the Newell schools); two became dentists; two medical doctors; another was the postmaster of Newell; and Ron, who was Ralph's and Rose's seventh son, became a physical therapist and later a hospital administrator in Elkins, West Virginia. "My father believed in educating the sons because he believed that the daughters would have husbands to take care of them, so we all pitched in the help educate the boys," said Joan LaNeve Martin.[30]

The Laneve family was a classic example of how many immigrant families came to the United States in the late 1800s and early 1900s. Appreciative of having work and a safe place to raise their families, they helped build the industrial might of the United States. They taught their children English, and instilled in them the American dream. Not hampered by the barriers of language, race, class, or ethnicity, the next generation was able to succeed in America and capture at least a piece of that dream.

The town grew so quickly that a brick school, the Fourth Street School was built in 1912 and graduated the first high school class of six students in 1916. Wells High School was built in 1927.[31]

During the 1920s and 1930s Homer Laughlin was under the leadership of W.E. Wells and Marcus Aaron, who had taken over for his father in 1911. Marcus also continued to live in Pittsburgh and was chauffeured to Newell every day by a driver who was also an accountant. During the day, the chauffeur would work in the accounting department and then drive Aaron home at night. Aaron was extremely active in education in Pittsburgh as the president of the Pittsburgh Board of Public Education from 1922 to 1942. In addition, he taught in the Religious School of the Rodef Shalom congregation, and was a trustee in that congregation for forty-four years. He remained as president of The Homer Laughlin China Company through 1940.[32]

The Homer Laughlin China Company took steps to maintain its dominant position in the American pottery industry by using modern technology to improve production methods. They conducted a nationwide search to find the most knowledgeable man in the country on pottery science. They found Dr. Albert Victor Bleininger, a professor of ceramics at Ohio State University. He was hired away from Ohio State in 1920 to become head of the research department at Homer Laughlin.[33]

Bleininger lived up to his reputation. In the previous decade Homer Laughlin had expanded the Newell plant and closed the East Liverpool operation, but demand for Homer Laughlin products encouraged the company to expand even further. They planned to build a new plant, called plant six, in vacant land south of the existing factory across a narrow creek valley. Bleininger was put in charge of building plant six which, when finished, was huge at 290 feet by 800 feet. However, the unique feature of the new plant was the use of tunnel kilns instead of the traditional bottle kilns. The tunnel kilns had a major advantage because they could be used continuously without having to wait for the kiln to cool down before it could be unloaded and used again like the bottle

Postcard view of the south front of Plant No. 4, The Homer Laughlin China Company taken before 1920. (Photo courtesy of The Homer Laughlin China Company)

kilns. In the new tunnel kilns, the ware was loaded into cars that conveyers carried through the kiln at fourteen feet an hour. Fifty-five hours later when the firing was complete, the ware emerged from the other end of the tunnel. The tunnel kiln ran continuously with ware in different stages of the firing process. The new plant also had a number of other industry advances in the mixing and preparation of the ingredients for making ware. The new plant was so innovative that it brought the pottery industry into the realm of modern manufacturing.

The tunnel kiln and the other innovations Bleininger developed were so successful that Homer Laughlin converted all of the Newell plants to tunnel kilns and the other new technologies. Demand for products remained so high that a plant seven was built in 1927 and plant eight in 1929, adjoining plant six and stretching south along the riverbank. Homer Laughlin reached a record payroll of 3,500 employees, more than half of whom still lived in East Liverpool and took the trolley to work each day in Newell. Homer Laughlin and Newell were the center of and the showplace of the American pottery industry.[34]

The Homer Laughlin management and financial operations were secure under W.E. Wells and Marcus Aaron. Its technology became the industry standard under Bleininger, but the company needed a design expert who could create innovative and unique designs for pottery. The company again hit the jackpot when Frederick Hurten Rhead was hired in 1927. Rhead was born in England into a family with a tradition of decorating pottery. Trained at art schools in England, he soon left to seek new opportunities in ceramic design in the United States. He worked as the art director of three different potteries in eastern Ohio before becoming a leading force at the prize-winning University City Pottery in St. Louis, where he built his reputation as one of the leading ceramics designers in the United States. Homer Laughlin hired him to be the company art director.[35] As Rhead began to settle in, Homer

Laughlin changed leadership in 1930 when W. E. Wells turned the secretary-treasurer and general manager positions over to his son, J.M. Wells, Sr., who would hold these positions for the next thirty years.

Although production was reduced somewhat during the early years of the Depression of the 1930s, the new management team—with Bleininger in charge of technology and Rhead creating new designs—drove Homer Laughlin to the peak of productivity during the next twenty years. Rhead's first major artistic success was the Virginia Rose pattern named for W.E. Wells' granddaughter. The pattern that featured a rose worked into the edge of the ware sold more than 600,000 dozen pieces at Woolworth's annually from 1933 until 1951.

However, Rhead's major accomplishment was the design of Fiesta® in 1936. Fiesta® is the most widely sold and collected of any of Homer Laughlin's products, and continues to be the largest selling American-made dinnerware. If I tell people that I am from Newell, West Virginia they give me a blank look, but if I mention Fiesta® it rings a bell with almost everyone.

Fiesta® is an art deco design, a style that became popular in the 1920s and 1930s. Art deco was used in the design of numerous products and buildings to denote a modern, streamlined break from traditional design. The Empire State Building is a classic example of an art deco building. The Fiesta® plates and saucers have thick concentric circles grooved to hold more glaze to create a blending with a slightly different hue on each circle. However, its most striking feature is the bright bold colors of the ware. The first colors were bright red, bright yellow, dark blue, and medium green. In addition to the main table setting, the company also marketed a number of accessories, including various sizes of candleholders, pitchers, and flower vases. Frederick Rhead called Fiesta® "the most successful line of tableware ever made in any factory anywhere."[36] Fiesta® screamed modernity and clearly placed Homer Laughlin

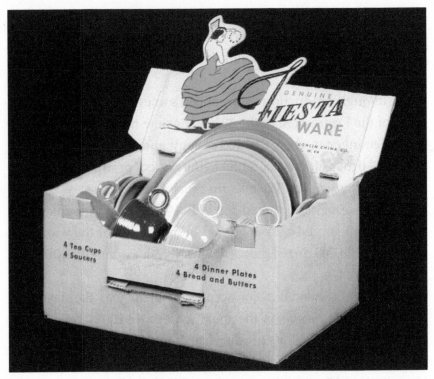

The Homer Laughlin China Company's best seller genuine Fiesta® (Advertisement courtesy of The Homer Laughlin China Company)

in the forefront of the American pottery industry in management, technology, and design.

In 1940 Marcus Lester Aaron was named to replace his father as the president of Homer Laughlin, a position he would hold for an astounding forty-eight years. Marcus Lester Aaron was educated at Princeton University and Harvard Law School, and like his grandfather and father before him he continued to live in Pittsburgh where he was a leader in the Jewish community, serving as the temple president of the Rodef Shalom synagogue from 1953 until 1973. He continued the family tradition of commuting daily from Pittsburgh to Newell to help run the pottery.[37]

"Mr. Aaron, who was the third generation family, basically

worked with my father. He was chauffeured from Pittsburgh five days a week. Mr. Aaron was a lawyer who never practiced law, so he not only advised on the financial side of the business but also helped us with legal matters," said Joseph Wells III.[38]

Homer Laughlin reached its highest level of production in 1941, when it produced 300,000 pieces of dinnerware per day. Production remained high during the war because of military contracts, one of which called for Homer Laughlin to supply 246,076 dozens of ware. Production was slowed somewhat by the labor shortage caused by men joining the armed services and pottery workers lured to higher paying defense jobs. To combat the shortage, Homer Laughlin gave the remaining potters double shifts and hired high school kids to work a shift after school. Women were also a key in war-time production. Twenty-five percent of the employees before the war were women, an extraordinarily high percentage of female workers for a manufacturing company. During the war Homer Laughlin hired even more women to work in what had traditionally been men's jobs.

The National Brotherhood of Potters, which had been a notoriously weak union, was even able to wrest some benefits from the companies with the help of the War Labor Board. In December 1945, the War Labor Board required that all pottery workers with one year of experience receive a one-week paid vacation, and workers with five years receive a two-week vacation. This was the first paid vacation in the history of the American pottery industry. That same agreement also paid workers overtime pay for more than eight hours' work and guaranteed women a minimum hourly rate of fifty-five cents an hour.[39]

The immediate post-World War II era was a time of prosperity for Newell as it was for the rest of industrial America. Employment and optimism in Newell were at an all-time high. Life was good and the future looked bright.

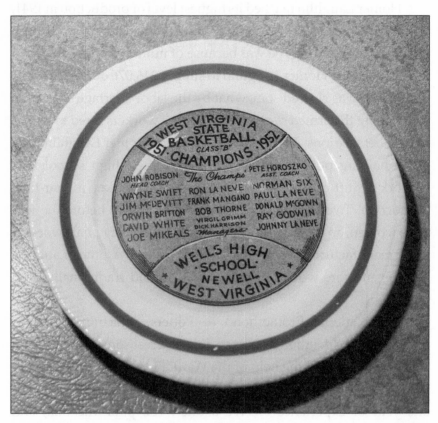

One of the commemorative plates made to honor the Wells High School state championship team. (Photograph by Michael Keller courtesy of *Goldenseal Magazine*)

Chapter 4

The Championship Season

Newell did not have many claims to fame. We were the home of the largest pottery in the whole world and the closest town to Waterford Park racetrack (now Mountaineer Resort and Gaming Center), although Chester, our bitter rival, was given credit for that because they were incorporated and Newell was not. But there was one thing that did set Newell apart from the hundreds of other small towns in West Virginia in the 1950s: we were the home of the 1951 - 52 West Virginia State High School Basketball Champions. For one glorious season, we were, and will forever be, number one.

When I moved from Follansbee to Newell in the spring of second grade, we lived in the lower end of town, a block from the high school and right next to the lower end playground that had one of Newell's three dirt basketball courts. That court was the center of basketball action in Newell. On weekends and in the evenings after high school baseball practice, the court was mobbed with high school and junior high kids and sometimes old, married men trying to recapture a sliver of their youth, even if just for a moment.

Because Follansbee was a football town, I had never played basketball, but I was intrigued by the game's action and the tremendous interest shown by the Newell kids. The big kids let me try to shoot, but I could barely get the ball to the rim, even throwing it underhand with both hands. I never got to play in any real games and had to be content with shooting around. The next year I was able to play in some games, at least until enough big kids came to form two full teams.

During the spring's rainy season, the court became a quagmire. On those occasions the high school boys would drive a couple blocks to a pottery shed to get bags of sawdust. Usually three or four bags of sawdust poured in the mud would improve the court, but often puddles remained on the court's edges. Five or six errant passes, a couple of dribbles off the foot, and a long rebound were enough for everyone to be covered head to foot by a damp, tan

Cheerleaders Joby Young, left, and Pat Gilmore smile for the camera while the boys practice on a dirt court on Washington Street in Newell in the early 1950s. (Photo courtesy of Joby Young Laneve and *Goldenseal Magazine*)

mud. By noon the court dried off and so did we, but we had to go home and face some irate mothers. In the summer the court would become extremely dry and dusty, but we could brush the dust off before we went home.

—

Occasionally a small high school will have an exceptional group of athletes at the same time. The legendary Carr Creek High School which had only seven boys in the high school but was Kentucky state basketball runner-up in 1928; the Waterloo Wonders, from a tiny high school in Appalachian Ohio, had two undefeated seasons and won state championships in Ohio in the 1930s; and of course Milan, Indiana, of the movie *Hoosiers*, which won the Indiana all class championship in the 1950s, all fit that category. Newell High school ranked with that trio of famous teams. With a high school of about 120 students, Newell easily qualified as being a small high school. The players on the 1951 - 52 Newell team were exceptional athletes. "We had some good athletes and shooters. Actually we were seven or eight deep with good athletes," John Laneve said. "And our only recreation then was playing basketball and baseball. There was a dirt court across the alley from my house, where I played in elementary and junior high school before they built the American Legion. We would burn tires to keep warm when we played on cold winter days and went home with that black smoke all over us."

Ron LaNeve (6'1"), a shooting forward, was clearly the best player. He was the second leading scorer in the state in West Virginia Class B that season, averaging twenty-five points per game. Norm Six (6'3"—215 pounds), the center, was big, strong, and agile. Six and guard Frank Mangano (6'1"—195 pounds) were outstanding football players who used their strength and size to clear out under the basket. The two juniors on the team were Ron's cousin, forward John Laneve (5'11"), an excellent defender who could shoot, and Jim

McDevitt (5'9"), a quick point guard. The previous year they had advanced all the way to the Class B Northern Area finals only to be beaten by Fairview High School, one game short of the state finals. With Newell losing only two players from that team, everyone had high hopes for this season.

As expected, Newell won the first two games of the 1951 - 52 season, beating Salineville (Ohio) High School 66 - 46 and Irondale (Ohio) High School 77 - 39, but was upset in the third game by our hated rivals, the Chester High School Panthers. "Frank [Mangano] was in the hospital with appendicitis. I don't know if that's why we lost or if they just ran us," recalled Norm Six. "After that game Robbie [Coach Robison] started running us hard in practice. The next time we played Chester we had them down twenty-five points by the end of the third quarter, and beat them easily."

The strongest team that Newell played was Wellsville, Ohio, led by the legendary, sharp-shooting, six-foot, nine-inch Clarence "Bevo" Francis. Bevo was an instant legend because it was rare for a big man to be able to both run and shoot. Many people considered him to be a freak because he was so tall, but he could play basketball. The next two seasons Bevo attended tiny Rio Grande College in Ohio, where he scored more than 100 points in a couple of games and led the Rio Grande Redmen to a national ranking.

Newell played against Bevo at Wellsville in the eighth game of the season. Norm Six recalled Newell's strategy for that game: "I did not play against many players taller than me. But Bevo was taller and he could shoot. The best strategy was to keep him from getting the ball. In the first game against Wellsville we tried to slow the game down and play a 1 - 3 - 1 zone defense. I played behind Bevo. The halftime score was Wellsville 11 - 9, but that forced us to play catch-up in the second half and we lost by sixteen points (17 - 33)." Recently, Ron LaNeve said, "After that game Newt Oliver, their coach, complained that Bevo was not able to get his shots and points, because we slowed the game down."

I went to every home game that year because I lived so close to the high school. My game night routine was always the same. Eat dinner. Get fifty-five cents because admission was thirty-five cents, and I always took an extra twenty cents for popcorn and a coke. Leave the house by 6:15. Run all the way to the high school to be first in line when the doors opened at 6:30. Race from the door to the front row middle seat, the same seat I occupied for every game but one.

The second game against Wellsville was different from other home games. Because of Bevo's reputation, and because Newell had such a strong team, this game was the featured game in the area that night. Although I anticipated a large crowd and left home twenty minutes before my usual time, to my surprise there were about twenty people already in line. Like many high schools of that era Newell had a combination gymnasium/auditorium facility which had been built as a New Deal project during the late 1930s and early 1940s. The basketball floor was on a large stage, about four feet above a band pit about twenty feet wide, and then came auditorium seating for 500 or 600 spectators. Above the auditorium seating was a balcony used by the band.

When I ran to my usual seat I found rows of folding chairs had been set up in the band pit, and the balcony was open to accommodate the overflow crowd. The best that I could do was to get a front-row folding chair, but it was at the foul line. That was a bad omen.

Newell abandoned the slow-down strategy that had not worked in the first meeting, but still lost. "We ran with them and were ahead at the end of the third quarter," recalled Norm Six. "But they hit ten of eleven shots in the fourth quarter and won the game."

The high point of the regular season came late in the year.

Newell was scheduled to play Class "A" powers Weirton (WV) High School, Moundsville (WV) High School, and Salineville a small Ohio high school. Newell needed to win all three games to have momentum going into the tournament. The Sweetheart Prom was also scheduled for the Saturday night of that week and the players wanted to go to the dance.

"We had a 10:00 curfew every night all season. Robbie wasn't going to let us go to the dance, because it would keep us out too late. But Frank Mangano talked to him and made a deal that if we won all three games we could go to the dance," said Norm Six. Newell easily beat Weirton 72 - 53, Moundsville 59 - 47, and Salineville 88 - 51. The victories over the big schools were important. "Beating Weirton and Moundsville really gave us confidence because we beat the big boys, the Class A schools," John Laneve said. "After the game the Weirton coach came to our dressing room and told us, 'Congratulations, you have a great team, but we are never going to play you again. You are so small that we don't have anything to win.'"

"We won them all and went to the dance, but when Robbie found out that we stayed out after midnight following the dance, he wasn't going to let us play the next week. He thought that we would just go to the dance and be home by 11:00. But Frank talked him out of that too. Frank was a real salesman," recalled Norm Six.

Newell ended the regular season with an outstanding 16 win 3 loss record and began tournament play led by John Laneve's twenty-eight points to crush New Cumberland High School by the score of 89 - 27. The trip to the state tournament was a triumphal march south, but when you are one of the northernmost high school in the state, in what other direction can you go? Each weekend of winning games took the Newell Big Green farther from home, but the Newell fans loyally followed the team. A caravan of cars traveled to every game, and the fans that had to stay at home listened eagerly to the radio broadcast on WOHI, the radio station in East Liverpool. At Grace's Place, a snack bar-confectionary on Washington Street in the heart of Newell's business district, owner Grace McCall kept a quarter-by-quarter, running score of each game in big numbers on the store's front window.

The Big Green rolled. They easily beat Pennsboro High School (63 - 50) and Sistersville High School (73 - 60) in the regional tournament at Williamstown. The week after the regional tournament, John Laneve and Joby Young, a junior cheerleader, began a classic basketball player-cheerleader romance. "John and I started dating two weeks before the championship game. He always bet milkshakes on the games and I had to buy him one at Carnahan's Drug Store. After the milkshake he headed down the alley toward home, but Ron (LaNeve) who was with us said that John had to walk me home. He did and we have been together for fifty-eight years since then," recalled Joby.

The Northern Area Tournament in Clarksburg was more of a challenge. In 1951 - 52 only the winners of the Northern and Southern Area tournaments went to the state finals. Newell beat Moorefield High School in a 67 - 51 romp, but had a more difficult time defeating Tygarts Valley High School, 58 - 51, to win the Northern Area championship and secure a state championship berth.

Paul LaNeve, Ron's brother, still remembers the thrill of the Northern Area Tournament games for him as a sophomore. "I played on the reserve team all season, but Robbie added Joe Michaels and me to the varsity for the tournament. I liked to travel to the games because the guys were just such great people to be with, but I especially liked the area tournament because Robbie put me in at the end of both games. It was only a minute each game, but I was really excited just to get in the games."

The state champion game against the Gassaway High School

Elks was set for Friday, March 21, 1952, at the West Virginia University Field House in Morgantown. Marilyn Gibas, a fifth grader who lived on Grant Street in Newell, but went to St. Aloysius Elementary School in East Liverpool, went to every tournament game. "My dad was a huge fan, so he took me out of school to go to the games," recalled Marilyn. "We were excited because Wayne Swift and John Laneve lived on our block. I don't remember that we went in a caravan, but when we stopped at restaurants they were full of Newell people."

I was not so lucky and had to be content to listen to the tournament games on WOHI. But I begged my father to take me to the state championship at Morgantown. He could not get off work to go. But I was ecstatic on Tuesday of championship week when he told me he found a ride for me. Carnahan's Drug Store made a list of everyone who needed a ride to the game. My dad put my name on the list and Keith Wheatley, who worked with my dad, saw my name and agreed to take me with his family.

Along with 800 other excited Newell fans, we left early that Friday morning and, after driving through Washington, Pennsylvania which everyone in Newell called "Little Washington," and then through Uniontown, Pennsylvania the best route at that time, arrived in Morgantown, West Virginia in less than three hours. I don't remember much about the trip except that I used some of the dollar that my dad had given me to buy a hamburger, French fries, and a milkshake for lunch in a Morgantown restaurant.

The West Virginia University Field House was massive, and the bleachers all around the court were packed with 5,000 fans. The playing floor was an impossible jumble of lines because it was also used for crosscourt basketball, volleyball, badminton, and who knew what else. I did not know how the players could sort out the basketball boundaries from all the other marks. But they did just fine. The crowd, which seemed huge to me, did not seem to affect the Newell team. "The crowd was big but we had played before big crowds before during the season," recalled John Laneve. "Once we got out on the floor we were oblivious and did what we had to do."

The players had mixed feelings about the field house, however. Ron LaNeve explained, "The Field House in Morgantown had glass backboards. We had only played on glass backboards a couple of times. They gave you a different look at the basket on a shot. Everything felt different and a little scary with a big crowd and a whole section of sportswriters."

Gassaway High School was an equally small school located in Braxton County. Both schools were about the size of Milan, Indiana, the small town that was the model for the film *Hoosiers*, so the game was like Hoosiers meeting Hoosiers except that a small town was guaranteed to win. Nobody from Newell knew anything about Gassaway or even where it was located. "Down state" was all that anybody could say about Gassaway. But remember, Newell was so far north that we had to negotiate sixty miles of the Northern Panhandle of West Virginia just to get to the main part of the state. We considered anything past Moundsville to be the deep south.

The *Wheeling Intelligencer* picked the game as a tossup. With a 22 - 2 record, Gassaway was led by 6'4" center Gary Mullins, who, averaging twenty-five points a game, was a one-man team. He had scored forty-six of his team's fifty-three points in the area semifinal game, and scored thirty points to beat Glen Rogers High School in the Southern Area Tournament final. "One of the things Coach Robison said was we had to keep Gary Mullins' scoring total down," remembered Ron Laneve. "Norm Six had that job."

Gassaway's Gene Gay opened the scoring, but Jim McDevitt tied the game for Newell with a long set shot from the top of the foul circle. After an exchange of baskets, Gay put Gassaway ahead 5 - 4. But two goals by John Laneve and a goal by Ron LaNeve gave Newell a commanding 10 - 5 lead. By the end of the first quarter Newell was leading 16 - 11. Mullins valiantly tried to keep Gassaway in the game during the second quarter by scoring eleven points when Six had to sit on the bench with three fouls. But Ron LaNeve's shooting and a balanced attack took Newell to a 36 - 25 halftime lead.

Newell was able to penetrate Gassaway's zone for easy inside shots and was content to let Gassaway play as slowly as they wanted. The Big Green maintained a 44 - 33 lead at the end of the third quarter. After a couple quick baskets by Newell in the fourth quarter, Coach Robison began to clear the bench. As Wayne Swift, Orwin Britton, David White, Don McGown, and Ray Godwin entered the game, the Newell fans stood and began to chant, "We're running away with Gassaway, we're running away with Gassaway." The student section began singing "It's Newell High School," sung to the tune of and using most the words of the West Virginia University fight song. Our fight song was repeated three times and everyone was on their feet chanting, singing, and throwing confetti as the game ended in a 56 - 39 romp for Newell. Ron LaNeve led the Big Green scoring with twenty-one points, John Laneve had twelve points, and Jim McDevitt had ten points in one of his best games of the season. Mullins led Gassaway with twenty-one points. But Norm Six had kept him in check and controlled the boards, pulling down fifteen rebounds. Newell hit twenty-five of sixty-six shots for a respectable thirty-eight percent. Gassaway made only fourteen of forty-five shots (thirty-one percent).

"I was surprised how easy the championship game was," recalled Jim McDevitt. "It was the second easiest game we played in the tournaments. The strongest Class B teams were in the northern part of the state, and a lot of them could have beaten Gassaway."

I must include a sentimental sidebar, later shared with me by Gary Mullins' son, Todd, in response to an article in *Goldenseal*

Gary Mullins of Gassaway shoots a jump shot while being closely guarded by Norm Six of Newell in the 1951 - 52 West Virginia State Class B Championship game. Newell won the game 56 - 39. (*Dominion–News* photograph courtesy of *Goldenseal Magazine*)

Magazine. Todd wrote, "You see, my dad was Gary Mullins, the vaunted Gassaway High star whose containment was apparently the key to the Newell victory. He married his grade-school, high-school sweetheart (Linda McNary) from the neighboring town of Sutton in Braxton County. She was also at that game, by the way, and tells the story that they had worked it out that when he went on the floor and put his hand over his heart for the National Anthem; it meant he loved her."

During the awards ceremony after the game, Ron LaNeve and Frank Mangano were named to the All-Tournament team. Coach Robison was given the huge Class B championship trophy, and all the players on both teams were given small trophies and, as a special treat, a pint bottle of chocolate milk. I think I slept for most of the ride home; I was one tired third grader.

The celebration of the championship reflected the simplicity of the town. "When we got home they had a big truck up near the Newell Bridge for a parade. We got out of our cars and the team and cheerleaders got on that truck for a parade through town," said Ron LaNeve. "We didn't expect that, but it was really nice." On Monday the high school had an assembly to honor the team and coaches. At the end of the assembly, the whole student body formed a chain and snake danced the seven-block length of Washington Street and back. Mrs. Haynes, my third grade teacher, let my class go to the windows to watch.

When the question of a banquet came up, the team made a unique choice. "After we won the championship the players were given the choice of having a team meal at the restaurant of our choice, recalled Jim McDevitt. "We voted to eat at Frank Mangano's

The championship team, coaches and cheerleaders at the school assembly on the Monday following the championship game. (Photo courtesy of *Goldenseal Magazine*)

house because his mother made the best spaghetti. She cooked for three days and we had a legendary meal."

The Lion's Club gave Coach Robison $200 hidden in a lettuce seed packet, at the school's championship assembly, perhaps to signify green growth or seed money. Coach Robison almost pitched the packet, but in the nick of time Frank Mangano suggested he look inside first. The town gave the players commemorative plates, and because we were a pottery town, there were at least three different types. The championship plate that I own and display in our kitchen has the names of the coaches, players, and managers superimposed over the picture of a basketball. Another plate had a picture of the team, and a third had the scores of all the games. Susan McKenna Bebout later paid $55 to buy a Newell championship plate (the one with the team picture) at a pottery auction.

Winning that championship was a huge point of pride for the people of Newell. "Newell was just a small factory town and we were always treated as also-rans, not only by the state but by the communities around us," said Orwin Britton, a sub on the team, in a *Mountain State Hoops* article. "We were the only rallying point that I can remember for the town." "The people of the town were really proud," said Ron LaNeve. "They never treated us any differently, but we could tell that they really appreciated how we represented the town."

After a month, baseball season started and things seemed to get back to normal. But they were never really the same. The championship was always in the back of our minds. It meant that everyone in Newell realized we did things differently; we were special, and we were the state champions. For me and other young boys, the champs inspired us to believe that people from Newell could go out into the world and compete and win. We were inspired to believe that championships, athletic scholarships, and college degrees were all within the realm of possibility.

To the Parents:

This report indicates the pupil's progress in school subjects and in those desirable habits, abilities and attitudes of mind that make for wholesome living and good citizenship. The increased number of separate items on the report are meant to convey to the parent more specific information on individual progress and growth. In the use of this report form, it should be understood that ratings are based upon effort and ability of the individual pupil and not by comparison with others of the group.

Explanation of marks —

O — Outstanding.

S — Satisfactory.

I — Improving; indicates progress, but not yet satisfactory.

U — Unsatisfactory.

PROGRESS IN DESIRABLE HABITS AND ABILITIES

	Six Weeks Period					
	1	2	3	4	5	6
Health Habits						
1. Sits, stands, and walks correctly	S-	S	S	S	S	S	S
2. Gives attention to cleanliness of person, hair, nails, face, teeth	S	O	O	O	O	O	O-
3. Uses handkerchief when needed	S+	O	O	O	O-O	O-
4. Observes the 8-point health standards	S	O	O	O	O	O
Social Habits						
1. Works and plays cheerfully with others	S	O	O	O	O	O	O-
2. Obeys safety rules	S	O	O	O	O	O
3. Respects rights and property of others	S	O	O	O	O	O O
4. Is polite in speech and action	S	O	O	O	O	O
Work Habits						
1. Can take and follow directions	S	S	S+	S+	O	O	S+
2. Makes good use of time	S-	S+	O	O	O	S	S+
3. Works independently	S	S	O	O	O	O	O-
4. Completes work promptly	S-	S-	O	O	S	S	S
Attendance and Punctuality						
Days Present	30	26	30	22	16	4½
Days Absent	0	0	0	8	½	2 10	½
Times Tardy	0	0	0	0	0	0	0

PROGRESS IN SCHOOL SUBJECTS

	Six Weeks Period					
	1	2	3	4	5	6
Reading						
1. Reading readiness (for beginners)	I	I+	S	S+	S	S	S-
2. Is ready to read on grade level	I	I+	S	S	S	S	S-
3. Reads orally so listeners enjoy it	I	I+	S+	O	O-S	S
4. Works out new words independently	I	I+	S+	S+	O-S	S
5. Reads silently for meaning	I	S	S+	S+	O-	S	S
6. Avoids bad reading habits, such as						
a. Lip movement	S-	S	S	S	O	O	S
b. Pointing	S-	S	S	S	O	O	S
Language						
1. Speaks clearly in a pleasant voice	S	O	O	O	O	O	O-
2. Can retell stories well	O	O	O	O	O	O	O
3. Tries to correct common speech errors	S	S+	O	O	O	O	O-
4. Strives for correct written form	S-	S	S+	O	O-S	S
Writing						
1. Forms letters correctly	I	S-	S	S	S	I	I+
2. Writes neatly and legibly	S-	S-	S	S-	S-	I	I+
3. Writes his best in other work	S-	S-	S-	S-	S-	S-	S-
Spelling (Grades 2-3)						
1. Spells words correctly	I	O	S+	S	O-	S	S
2. Pronounces words distinctly	S	O	O	O	O	O
3. Observes correct spelling in all writing	S	O	O	O-O	O-O	O-
Numbers						
1. Knows number facts of the grade	S	S	S	S	S-	S	I+ S-
2. Uses number facts in everyday experiences	S	S	S	S	S	S	S
3. Reads carefully and thinks through problems	S	S	S	S	S	S	S
4. Works up to standard—						
a. Speed	S-	S-	S	S	S	S-	S-
b. Accuracy	S-	S-	S	S	S	S-	S-
Art						
1. Shows originality in expression	S	S	S	I	S-S	S-
2. Is neat and orderly	S-	S	S	S	S	S-	S-
Music						
1. Finds pleasure in singing	S	S	O	O	O	O	O
2. Shows sense of rhythm	S	S	S+	S	S	S	S
Group Activities (Social Studies and Science)						
1. Works well with other children on activity units	S	S	O	O	O	O	O-
2. Shows an interest in how people live and work and play together	S	S	O	O	O	O	O-
3. Is developing on acquaintance with nature	S	S+	S+	S	S	S	S+
4. Collects and brings in materials for nature and science	S	S+	S+	S	S	S	S+

My third grade report card as evidence that Mrs. Haynes was right when she passed me in third grade, instead of holding me back as she once suggested to my parents. Notice the high grades in health and social habits like "Uses handkerchief when needed," O-minus.

Chapter 5

School: A Shoe Shine and a Smile

I was every teacher's worst nightmare. I seemed bright and used good grammar, but when it came time to do the work I just didn't seem to be able to perform. My work was sloppy, my handwriting was almost illegible, I could not spell, I daydreamed constantly, and I did not like to read. I showed glimpses of ability when I got high scores on major tests, but then slid back into inability to produce on a daily basis.

If I were in elementary school today I would probably be diagnosed as having a learning disability. I had symptoms of dyslexia and attention deficit disorder, but could also have qualified for the gifted program. In the 1950s before learning disabilities were discovered and labeled, I was considered lazy and inattentive. School was a difficult adventure of trying to cope with finding where my talents lay and how to use them. Elementary school was a hard time for me.

When I moved to Newell I spent the last half of second grade in Newell's Fourth Street School, which was built in 1912. The Fourth Street School was an ancient red brick building with wooden floors that creaked when I walked on them. The desks were bolted to the floor and had inkwells on the top right-hand side despite the fact that ballpoint pens were quickly replacing fountain pens. The Fourth Street School smelled like a school, with a mixture of chalk dust, linseed oil used to clean the floors, and damp wool from too many children playing in the rain at recess. The school was so decrepit that during the school carnival that spring Mr. Johns, the principal, limited the number of people who could come into the building at any one time because he was afraid the floors would collapse.

The next year I was excited to start third grade in the brand new, modern Jefferson Elementary School, built next door to the old Fourth Street School. Jefferson Elementary School was a two-story light-colored brick classroom building. Each classroom was full of modern wonders like lockers along the inside wall for us to hang our coats and store our lunches and books. Every elementary school I had attended before had cloakrooms, separate rooms attached to the classroom that had hooks for us to hang our coats; this was also where we were sent as a punishment when we disrupted class. The new school had tile floors laid on concrete so the floors did not creak and the one-piece desks, made of light-colored metal and wood, could be moved easily. Everything looked bright and clean and smelled of fresh paint. I thought I was learning at the cutting edge of modern education in America.

The new school had a large room with a kitchen for a cafeteria, a new concept. None of us had ever gone to a school with a cafeteria that served hot food or any other kind of food for that matter, nor did we know anyone who had. A cafeteria seemed like a good idea to us. Kids who lived in town walked home for lunch, but the bus kids who comprised more than half of the school ate sack lunches in their classroom which wasn't much fun.

We got to use the new cafeteria for only one year The year

This was my fourth grade class from Jefferson Elementary School. My first girlfriend, Denise Bowen, is the cute girl in pigtails second from left in the first row. I'm third from left in the second row. My friends from the lower end of town: Sharon Haddox is fifth from the left in the second row, Sue Ellen Logston is on the far left in the third row, and Tom Woods is on the far right in fourth row. Ruth McCabe, who lived in the country, is fourth from the left in the top row.

after Jefferson Elementary School opened, the cafeteria had to be divided into two classrooms with a sliding door between them to accommodate the influx of students who were the first of the baby boomers, children born in the post-World War II period. The baby boomers came so fast that by 1955, when my brother started school, a third floor had to be added to Jefferson Elementary School.

Newell wasn't growing in adult population, but more kids were being produced, almost as if sex had been rationed during World War II along with butter and gasoline. When the war was over and the soldiers came home, they ate more butter, used more gasoline, and produced more babies. Many women continued to work after the war. Despite the belief that they would neglect their home duties, the post-war baby boom seemed to prove that working women of that era were not. A boom crop of kids was born in the late 1940s and early 1950s.

Our new school was bright and modern, but the teachers were the same ones who had been in the old building. Most of the elementary kids loved the elementary teachers and hugged them and walked with them down to the crosswalk at Washington Street at noon and after school, but I thought the teachers were a quirky lot to be avoided as much as possible. In our young minds, all the teachers seemed middle-aged, but could have been anywhere from their 20s to their 50s. Back then, people tried to look older and more mature as opposed to everyone trying to look younger as they do in today's world.

My most memorable teacher was Mrs. Haynes, my third grade teacher; we clashed from the very first day of school. She was a tall, no-nonsense lady who bore a striking resemblance to the "Church Lady" character later made famous on *Saturday Night Live*. She believed in being very formal in the third-grade classroom. She insisted on calling us by our proper names. "Clarence, do you know the answer?" she would ask looking directly at me. No one ever called me Clarence so I ignored her for the first three weeks. For the next three weeks she tried my middle name. "What do you think, Robert?" she inquired, again looking directly at me. Of course I did not answer because my name was Bobby. She thought I was deaf or slow. My report card at the end of the first grading period had a bunch of *I*s, "improving, but not satisfactory." After a six-week battle of wills, we both realized this was not helping either of us so we struck a truce when she agreed to call me Bob if I would answer when she called my name.

Even after I started to answer questions, it was clear that Mrs. Haynes thought I would not amount to much. The things the teachers at Jefferson Elementary School valued most were neat

My most memorable teacher was Mrs. Haynes my third grade teacher; we clashed from the very first day of school. (Photo from *The History of Newell and Vicinity*, reprinted by The Tri-State Genealogical & Historical Society, 1995)

handwriting, good spelling, paying attention, and following the rules. After all, those were the very things that had enabled the teachers to rise from the ranks of factory workers to their exalted posts as elementary school teachers. I had pretty well established myself as an inattentive rule-breaker during our battle over my name. Unfortunately, I was also bad at spelling. My handwriting was worse. My goal in writing was to get it done fast, and making neat little loops and perfect push-pull strokes slowed me down too much. Every paper came back covered in red circles around the misspelled words and with a big red SLOPPY written across the front.

Mrs. Haynes assigned seats based on how smart she thought we were. The smartest kids got seats in rows to her left as she faced the class. The rest of us sat in order of descending IQs. She usually grudgingly placed me somewhere near the middle of the class because of my test performance. On the six-week tests, I frequently astonished her by getting one of the highest grades in the class; but she chalked it up to blind luck and did not really change her view of my abilities. She didn't consider test scores to be important. What counted with her were the daily worksheets and fill-in-the-blank exercises from our workbooks; she believed that students who cranked those out with ease were the bright ones. I was clearly not one of those. In fact, Mrs. Haynes suggested to my parents that I should be retained in third grade. My parents nixed the idea of holding me back and I was promoted, but it was a close call.

Mrs. Haynes did have a lasting effect on me. She frequently told us that, "You can go anywhere in life if you have a shoe shine and a smile." I soon found out that you needed more than a shoe shine and a smile to get anywhere and began to question everything I had learned in elementary school.

Of course, there were other memorable teachers. Miss Laneve, our writing teacher, believed that penmanship was an art. She made us perform hundreds of exercises in which we wrote only parts of letters. For weeks on end, we drew only the first stem of the letter W. How I longed to write a complete W. We were thrilled to have Mrs. Highfield, the geography teacher and the most technologically savvy member of the faculty because she showed us movies about people from foreign lands. Without those movies many of us would not have realized that people who live in tropical climates are primitive because it is too hot to do any work.

Miss Moore was the most exciting teacher because she was

dating the principal, Mr. Johns. Once I saw him and Miss Moore driving in his car, with her sitting very close to him in the front seat. I waved and she waved back, somewhat sheepishly, I thought. Miss Moore, a middle-aged spelling and language teacher, was a tall woman who towered over the painfully short Mr. Johns. In pictures of the Jefferson Elementary School faculty, Mr. Johns can be seen standing on a step, so that he would be as tall as the women teachers standing on the floor. The two never married. One of his male colleagues quoted Mr. Johns as saying, "Why buy the cow when you can get the milk free?" I don't think he did much milking though. He lived in Chester with his unmarried sisters.

One of the best teachers at Jefferson Elementary School was Vera Osborn Nease who loved teaching so much that she once resorted to subterfuge to stay in the classroom. Vera, who taught my brother and sister in first grade and was the mother of my friends Carol and Mary Nease, came from a family of educators.

Her father, A.D. Osborne, was a school superintendent and a high school teacher until his untimely death in 1935. His resourceful widow, Annie Osborne, turned their home into a rooming house catering to unmarried teachers so that she and her children could survive the Depression.

Born in East Liverpool in 1903, Vera Osborne became a teacher in 1921, as soon as she graduated from Newell High School. Her initial jobs were in the Warren, Ohio and East Liverpool schools, but she returned to Newell to teach history at the Fourth Street building. Picking up courses at night and in the summer from area colleges, she was finally able to graduate from Geneva College in Pennsylvania in 1937.

In 1938 she fell in love with and decided to marry Clarence Nease, a much younger man who owned the Esso gas station in Newell. The only thing holding the marriage back was that Vera would have to quit her teaching job if they got married. Married women were not allowed to teach, because school boards then believed that women should be home taking care of their husbands and families, and not out in the world teaching young children. Occasionally couples like my Aunt Bess and Uncle Jim Miller got married and kept the marriage secret so the wife could keep teaching, but that was difficult to do in small towns. Uncle Jim and Aunt Bess's secret lasted only one semester before she resigned from her teaching position.

Vera and Clarence, who secretly married in 1938, were much better at keeping secrets. Clarence continued to live with his parents on Grant Street, two blocks from Vera's home on Washington Street. While Vera lived with her mother the couple spent a lot of time at the Nease house on Grant Street because it offered more privacy than the Osborne boarding house. Very discreet, they were able to keep the marriage secret for more than three years. What finally gave the secret away was Vera's pregnancy with their first child, Carol, who was born in 1941. Vera remained at home for a few years and Mary, their second daughter, was born in 1943.

But, in 1945, when Mary was two years old, Hancock County Schools removed the ban on married women teaching because there was a critical wartime shortage of teachers. The principal at the Fourth Street School begged Vera to come back to teach, which she was glad to do.

My brother Jimmy was in Mrs. Nease's first grade class. She caught him and his best friend David trying to cheat near the end of the school year. Jimmy was trying to keep his friend from flunking first grade by giving him signals for the correct answers on a multiple-choice test. Of course Mrs. Nease caught them. How slick could first graders be at cheating, particularly when one was failing? Mrs. Nease sent them out into the hall, where she then confronted two very scared first graders. Of course they both confessed because Mrs. Nease was so nice about the way she reprimanded them. She let them off with a stern warning, which they both took to heart,

Vera and Clarence Nease married in 1938 but kept their marriage secret so that she could keep her teaching job. (Photo courtesy of Mary Nease Brandal)

never cheating again. She flunked David because he was not ready to move on to second grade, but he still liked Mrs. Nease so much that he asked to be in her class again.

Mrs. Nease retired from teaching in 1968 because West Virginia had mandatory retirement at age sixty-five. With her love for teaching, she took a job across the river in the East Liverpool schools where she taught six more years before she finally retired, ending a forty-two-year career.

Most of the elementary teachers had grown up in Newell and had never been anywhere else except perhaps to go away to a teachers' college in an equally small town in the summer. They came from working-class backgrounds and taught the values of working hard, putting in a full day's work, and following the rules. Their lives and their teaching emphasized making the best of your lot, and of course putting a smile on your face and keeping your shoes shined.

In sixth grade my class was sent to the high school building because the first grade had enough baby boomers to make three classes instead of the usual two and there was no room for the sixth grade at Jefferson Elementary School. The twelve-room high school was built in 1926 on land given by The Homer Laughlin China Company and was originally called Wells High School

W.E. Wells after whom Wells High School was named. By the mid-1950s the name Newell High School came into common usage. (Photo courtesy of The Homer Laughlin China Company)

after one of the owners of the pottery, W.E. Wells. By the mid-1950s, we referred to it as Newell High School. The high school was an attractive two-story U-shaped building set back from Washington Street with pleasant front and side lawns and ivy clinging to its walls. A combination gymnasium and auditorium was added in the early 1940s as part of a Depression-era public works project. Our football field was next to the school along Washington Street and our baseball field, Clarke Field, was across Washington Street. Newell had the best baseball, football, and basketball facilities of any small school in the area. The junior high school, grades seven and eight, used the same building and shared some of the teachers with the high school.

⟶

Junior high school was both better and worse than elementary school. We were in the same building with the high school, where we had physical education class, football and basketball teams, dances, and high school plays and programs. All of that was really cool. On the other side of the coin, our teachers in elementary school were nurturing, but our teachers in junior high school were more like instructors. They expected us to perform in the classroom and weren't afraid to give us Cs, Ds, and occasionally Fs to spur us along.

Junior high was an awkward time for many of us because we were going through early adolescence, that twilight time between childhood and becoming an adult. I still wanted to play children's games, but was also having strange feelings toward girls. I knew I wanted to play hide-and-seek with them, but I did not know what to do when we hid. My parents wanted me to show more adult behavior but still treated me like a child, setting up a confusing array of rules. My voice and my body were changing and my hormones were running amok. Kids in my class like Bill Moffitt, Larry Hutton, and Sue Ellen Logston adjusted well to junior high

Newell High School was an attractive, two-story U-shaped building set back from Washington Street with pleasant front and side lawns and ivy clinging to its walls. (Photo 1958 Newell High School Yearbook)

school and continued to do well academically. I continued to be a very average student, somewhat grumpy with mercurial mood swings that made me difficult to be around.

Junior high was also the time when students begin to drop out of school. The legal age for quitting school in West Virginia was sixteen years old, so students who had failed a couple grades in elementary school began to turn sixteen in seventh or eighth grade. The first of my classmates to quit school was Sylvia Lupino who quit school at the end of sixth grade, at age fourteen, to get married. Apparently, girls could drop out at any age to get married.

Sue Ellen Logston's mother took Sue Ellen and her friend Sharon Haddox to Chester during the summer to visit Sylvia in her small apartment over a dry cleaning store. They reported that the apartment was very nice and Sylvia seemed to be happy. None of the rest of us ever saw her again.

Monk Owens, my second classmate to drop out, quit school in the middle of seventh grade on his sixteenth birthday. Our teachers told us we would have trouble getting a job without a high school diploma and said that we could not even get a job in the pottery. Ironically, when I went to work at my summer job in the pottery, Monk was the first person I saw there.

One of the most heartbreaking casualties of my junior high school experience in Newell was Deuce Dunlevy. Deuce was a prototype for Fonzie, the hip character on the television show *Happy Days*. Deuce wore leather jackets and T-shirts, had a beautiful ducktail haircut he combed frequently, and seemed to know everything hip. Deuce was polite to teachers, older people, and women. Unlike the Fonz, Deuce did not deliver memorable sayings nor give sage advice.

A grade ahead of us in elementary school, Deuce was an excellent athlete, good enough in Little League baseball to be picked for the East Liverpool League all-star team. Sadly, he never played junior high basketball despite being six feet tall and well-coordinated. Deuce earned an *F* or two on every six-week junior high report card, which was enough to keep him off the team. We were really surprised because, while the junior high teachers gave students *C*s and *D*s, they rarely gave an *F* unless you caused trouble, and Deuce wasn't a troublemaker. I don't know if he really was dumb or just so stubborn that he would not do anything. Deuce was not one of those athletes who had been held back two or three grades and was sixteen in the eighth grade. Every junior high school team had a couple of those guys who with two extra years of maturity were able to dominate junior high sports. But they would fizzle out when they moved up to high school the next year and began to play with kids their own age. Deuce had never failed a grade and was the same age as the rest of the kids in his class.

For two years Deuce sat in the stands and watched us far less talented players go down to defeat at the hands of other junior high school basketball teams. The only satisfaction he got was on weekends, when we played on the dirt basketball courts around town. Deuce soundly beat us in games. All the while he would describe and demonstrate what he would have done to "that big number 42" if he had been in the game.

Deuce finally got his chance for athletic glory when he was a freshman in high school. He passed enough classes to be promoted to high school, which made him eligible to play high school sports, at least until the first grading period ended. Deuce made the most of his opportunity. He tried out for fullback on the varsity football team, but could not beat out a senior who held the position. He was the second team varsity fullback. Newell High School was almost too small to field a football team. At 6'1" and 165 pounds, Deuce had too much size as well as too much talent to waste on the bench, so the coach made him the starting guard on the first team varsity, where he played extremely good, if not outstanding, football. A freshman in the starting lineup at the beginning of the season was virtually unheard of in Newell. In the history of the high school, Newell had had three or four football players who earned college football scholarships, and only one of them had started as a high school freshman.

Deuce was even better as the fullback on the junior varsity team. The Newell football team usually had only twenty or thirty players ranging from freshmen through seniors. But every year we had a junior varsity schedule of three or four games. The junior varsity team consisted of all the freshmen, sophomores, and juniors who were not on the starting team. Sometimes there were as few as twelve players on the junior varsity team. A freshman team was out of the question because we never had enough freshmen to make a football team and almost didn't have enough players for a freshman basketball team. The junior varsity was great experience because everyone who stayed on the team got to play in some games, and some guys like Deuce played two games a week.

The varsity games were played on Friday night and the junior varsity games were played on Monday after school. During that fall of 1956 Deuce started on the varsity at guard on Friday nights and at fullback on the JV team on Monday afternoon. He did a good job in varsity games, but dominated the JV games just as he bragged he would. He had a couple of JV games in which he gained more than a hundred yards and scored two or three touchdowns running from the fullback position. He was a man among boys.

Deuce was as relaxed and happy as I had ever seen him, but was almost too cool to show his pleasure at finally getting his chance and making good. We believed he had a bright future ahead in football. We envisioned scholarship offers to West Virginia University, maybe Virginia Tech, Pitt, or perhaps even the legendary Notre Dame. A pro football career didn't seem to be out of the question. After every game we hung out on the corner while Deuce regaled us with stories about what it was like to play in varsity football games and what he hoped to do when he got to be a junior and senior and beyond. That was a golden fall, a beautiful time for him and for those of us who were his friends and could dream with him.

Then, just before the seventh game of the season, report cards came out. Again Deuce did not pass enough classes to keep playing. We were shocked. We thought for sure he had learned his lesson in junior high and would work hard enough to pass. Even if he didn't pass, wouldn't the teachers take pity on a football star and pass him through? Or wouldn't the coaches intercede on his behalf to keep him on the field? The answer to both questions was no. We quickly learned that no matter how good an athlete was, our high school teachers and coaches expected passing grades to be earned and the coaches in Newell would never ask a teacher to pass an athlete just so he could play.

We never knew exactly how many classes Deuce failed. He quietly turned in his uniform that afternoon, and never played another minute of high school sports.

Deuce stayed in school that year, but he seemed to hang out on the street corner more and attend school less often. That summer and the next he played on the Globe Brick Company Prep League baseball team (a youth baseball league for boys fifteen to seventeen), but his heart wasn't in it. Deuce quit school and joined the Marines at the end of that second summer. He came home after basic training during the Christmas break, as cool as ever. His ducktail haircut had been replaced with a short Marine haircut, and he had some great stories about his Marine experiences. But he seemed a little subdued. He should have been a high school junior who had just finished his third season of football and was starting basketball season. Instead, he had passed through the doorway of adulthood and what he saw didn't match his dreams on the other side.

The Marines sent Deuce to Okinawa where he was a truck driver. Barely seven months later, we heard that he had been killed in a truck accident. We really weren't surprised. He easily fit the role of one of the "live fast, die young" rebels, like James Dean.

Newell did not have a funeral home. Instead of Chester or East Liverpool, both only a mile away, Deuce's funeral was held at the Turley Funeral Home in New Cumberland, which was twelve miles from Newell. Nevertheless, several of us got dressed up and went to the viewing of the body the night before the funeral. Deuce was decked out in that really sharp Marine dress uniform. The body was Deuce's, but his face looked brown and wax-like. It wasn't the Deuce we knew.

None of us went back to New Cumberland for the funeral,

because it was during the day and most of us had to work on summer jobs. Deuce was the first person in our age group to die, but strangely enough his death did not cause us to ponder our own mortality or reduce our adolescent sense of invincibility. I think we felt Deuce had reached his peak in that golden fall of 1956 when he burned so brightly for a short time, like a comet. We could not imagine Deuce as an aging adult working in the pottery, repeating stories of how he could have been great. Plus, it was summer and we had dates to go on, dances to go to, and two more years of high school.

My favorite things to do in high school, in order of interest, were playing sports, chasing girls, reading, and writing term papers. My interests are reflected in this book because there are four chapters on sports, two on dances, and only one on school.

My third most favorite thing to do in school was read. Starting in sixth grade, I became a voracious reader. But that hadn't always been true. Through the first five-and-a-half years of school I absolutely hated reading. I read only the minimum number of book-report books required to pass for the year, which was usually one every six weeks. I would finish the year with maybe seven, eight, or nine book reports, while the book sharks like Mary Huff, Mary Nease, Larry Hutton, and Bill Moffitt would have thirty or forty. For each book report we wrote or gave orally, we got a book sticker on a big chart in the back of the classroom. The lines on the chart after their names looked like library shelves, but mine looked like most of the books had been checked out.

What turned the tide for me was *Lassie Come Home,* written by Eric Knight. I had checked the book out from the class library even though it was a huge book with multiple chapters and was about a dog. I did not like long, chapter books and never liked dogs after being bitten by one when I was five, so I don't know what possessed me to check out that book. My taste ran to books about sports (of which there were none in our small, sixth-grade library), books about Disney characters, or the shortest books on the shelf with lots of pictures. Though I had *Lassie Come Home* checked out for two weeks, I had not read a single page when my teacher, Mr. LaNeve, said I had to either read it or turn it in. Reluctantly I started to read. In the first couple of chapters I fell in love with Lassie, and that was even before the television show existed. Then, when Lassie was taken to a remote area in Scotland, a place so far from her home in England that it would be impossible for her to return, I became transfixed by her homeward journey. I began to read in every spare moment, even with a flashlight under the covers at night. I finished the book in four days and was hooked on reading for life.

In seventh grade my cousin Bob Gracey gave me his extensive collection of young adult books that included an almost complete set of the Hardy Boys books with a few Chip Hilton books thrown in. The Hardy Boys stories were a series of more than thirty-five fiction books, written by various ghostwriters under the name Franklin Dixon. Aimed at a young adult audience they featured Frank and Joe Hardy, ages sixteen and fifteen respectively, who were the sons of ace detective Fenton Hardy, from Bayport. In each of the books the brothers and their cast of friends solve some kind of mystery or crime. I started with the *Wailing Siren Mystery*, which made me want to read more, but my favorite of all the Hardy Boys Stories was *The Secret of the Lost Tunnel*. In it Joe and Frank traveled to a Civil War battlefield in the south where they found lost Confederate gold disguised as cannon balls. I loved that story because of the rich descriptions of languid southern days under trees with Spanish moss and eating fried chicken and lacy pancakes. But I really liked the series because adults in the story actually respected the boys' judgment and ability.

My best friend, Larry Hutton, also became a Hardy Boys fan when I loaned him *The Secret of the Lost Tunnel*. We worked our way through each book in the series, even buying the ones that were missing from Bob Gracey's collection. We discussed and criticized each book and the characters in it, but never in the presence of our non-reading friends, who would have made fun of us.

After finishing the Hardy Boys we started the Chip Hilton series. Written by West Virginia native Clair Bee in the 1940s and 1950s, each book focuses on one sport season during the high school and college career of the fictional Chip Hilton. Bee turned out a total of twenty-three Chip Hilton books between 1948 and 1965.

We read every one up to number thirteen, *Fourth Down Showdown*, during our eighth grade summer, when we were absorbed with playing sports. We had to buy those books because the Bob Gracey collection had only three Chip Hiltons. Larry and I would each buy a book and then trade so we got to read two books for the price of one. *Fourth Down Showdown* was my favorite. It was a typical Chip Hilton story in which Chip and his pals were sophomore football players at State University. After a promising victory in their first game, Chip and his friends stayed out after team curfew to help an at-risk kid who worked at the drugstore with Chip. Chip and his friends turned themselves into the coach for curfew violation, but refused to make excuses for why they were out late. They were suspended from the next game, but reinstated when the family of the boy Chip befriended explained the circumstances to the coach. Chip and his friends learned of their reinstatement while listening to the radio broadcast of the away game. They drove across the state to arrive just in time for the final play, a trick play they had devised on the trip to the game. The play worked and State U won the big game. In this, as in all of the series, Chip takes the high road and everything turns out for the best. Later, when I studied Plato and Platonic idealism, I often thought of Chip Hilton, the ideal heroic figure who always made the morally correct decision even in the face of severe opposition.

Larry and I read every sports book in the Newell High School library. My particular favorite was *The Phantoms of the Foul Line*, a novel that featured Mickey Barton, a five-foot, five-inch high school and college basketball player. I loved this book because I was almost the same height as Mickey and I could relate to the problems he faced as an undersized basketball player. At the end of the book, Mickey stood at the foul line in the final seconds with the game on the line. Of course I dreamed I would be there sometime holding the game in my hands.

By the middle of our junior year Larry and I had read all the sports books, all the books about dogs, and the three or four car books in our small high school library. We even read a couple girls' books, hoping we could learn some secret techniques that would make us irresistible, but found them so boring we could barely finish them.

Then I made one of the most startling discoveries of my life. When I was doing research for my junior term paper at the Carnegie Library in East Liverpool, the librarian told me I could get a library card for free by merely completing the application. I was ecstatic, because they had thousands of books in their collection. Why hadn't my teachers or parents told me about this before?

At first I did not know what to check out. The literature we studied in high school English was of little help because it consisted largely of short stories by writers like Poe and O. Henry and poetry such as "The Rime of the Ancient Mariner" and *Beowulf*. Because I would be taking world history as a senior, I began to check books out of the history section like William Shirer's *Berlin Diary*, which I really liked because it was about the prelude to World War II. For the rest of the summer I went to East Liverpool to check history books out of the library. Only later when I got to college would I learn about Hemingway, Fitzgerald, Steinbeck, and Conrad.

Since my father worked in East Liverpool, he often returned

the books for me. He always waited at the librarian's desk while she checked through the book to make sure I hadn't left anything in it. Once I had. I was using a picture of a semi-nude woman I had purchased at the penny arcade at Rock Springs Amusement Park and betting tickets from Waterford Park racetrack, where I was working, to mark my place. The librarian carefully removed the picture and each ticket one by one and handed them to my father, who, turned beet red and tried to stammer out an explanation. "I was never so embarrassed in my whole life," my father said that evening when he confronted me with the betting tickets and picture. The lecture that followed was so severe I did not have the courage to ask him to give the picture back.

~

Newell High School was very small, with between 140 and 200 students. It was so small that I had only thirty-five students in my senior class. The school survived as a high school until 1963 when Newell, Chester, and New Cumberland were consolidated into Oak Glen High School.

The Newell High School teachers were a cut above the elementary teachers. All of them were stable, middle-class family people who were well educated. Mr. Robison, the basketball coach/ math teacher, had a Master's degree from the prestigious Columbia University Teacher's College. Mrs. George and Miss Mountford had Master's degrees from the University of Pittsburgh. Mr. Slack and the principal, Mr. Gregory, had Master's degrees from West Virginia University. One reason Newell attracted good teachers was that Hancock County schools offered the highest pay of all fifty-five counties in West Virginia. The science teachers were the weak link in the system, because almost anyone with any science background could get a higher paying job in the steel mill.

I thought that one of the best teachers was Mrs. George, the American history/civics teacher who stood only five-feet tall, but could bring burly football linemen to tears with her sharp wit. I developed my love for history because of her classes. She was the senior class sponsor who ruled us with an iron hand and a sense of humor. She was also the keeper of the senior traditions and presided over events such as the senior banquet and the graduation ceremony. Everyone who ever had her for a teacher, and that included Larry Hutton's mom, who had been taught by Mrs. George twenty years before when she was much younger and named Miss Sloan, loved and respected her.

Mrs. Schilling, the junior and senior English teacher who taught us how to write term papers, was also exceptional. She was the junior class sponsor, came back to school two nights the week before the prom, and brought her new husband with her to help us decorate. When she was the cheerleader sponsor they once had a flat tire on a trip to a game. She got out in the snow and changed that flat tire wearing her new fur coat.

My parents had always drummed into me that I was going to go to college when I graduated from high school. But going into my junior year I did not even have a 2.0 grade point average. I had gotten by in elementary school because I knew more than most of the other kids and the lessons were easy. High school was different because I had to actually study and learn stuff. Still lazy and stubborn, I did not want to do either.

I had *D* averages in algebra and in both Latin I and Latin II. I hated Latin and never should have taken the second year after getting a *D* in Latin I. Mrs. Robison, the Latin teacher, passed me out of the goodness of her heart. Thank you, Mrs. Robison, wherever you are.

"If you don't get better grades, you are going to end up working in the pottery," my Dad said as he looked at one unusually bad report card. Even I was beginning to doubt my ability to make the grades in college. I thought I was smart enough, but the evidence was piling up that perhaps I was just a below-average student from a small high school destined, as my Dad said, to work in the pottery for the rest of my life.

During the first semester of my junior year an event occurred that changed my life forever. About half the members of our class, all the students in the college prep curriculum, took the ACT test. Standardized tests to determine college admissions and placement were just coming into widespread use in the 1950s, and Newell High School students had been taking the ACT test for just about six years. Mom drove me to Weirton High School about half an hour away to take the test on a Saturday morning. I did not think the test was very hard because it was mostly reading comprehension with multiple-choice answers. I thought the smart kids must have done really well.

The results of the test astounded the teachers. I had received the highest score ever recorded by a student at Newell High School. I was only a couple points away from winning a college scholarship. A special faculty meeting was called and my parents were summoned to discuss my scores. Some teachers thought I was just lucky, but the general consensus was I must be smart, but not working up to my capacity. My parents were thrilled with the results.

Robbie was the first to break the news to me, when he criticized me in front of the whole class for reading escapist literature before math class when I should have been reviewing the lesson for the day. "Barnett is just sitting there wasting his time dreaming that he is the phantom of the foul line when he should be checking his math homework," he said. Then he went on to lecture me in front of the class about wasting my time and the ability that I had shown on the ACT test. I wasn't angry, but felt proud that he recognized that I had ability.

The teachers all began to treat me differently. They prodded me with, "You can do better than that," and "Do that over the right way and turn it in tomorrow." Something worked, because over the next three semesters I improved my grades tremendously, getting B averages in plane geometry, physics, American history, principles of democracy, and world history, and C averages in all my other classes. I raised my final high school GPA to 2.20 and finished with a class rank of seventeen out of thirty-five graduates. I certainly didn't qualify for the National Honor Society, but at least I squeaked out of the bottom half of the class.

By tradition, the junior and senior English classes in Newell each spent six weeks writing a term paper under the direction of Mrs. Schilling, the upper level English teacher. The papers consisted of twenty pages of double-spaced, handwritten text, plus an introduction, footnotes, a summary, conclusions, and a bibliography. While this does not sound like something that would have appealed to me, quite the opposite was true.

I absolutely loved researching and writing term papers with the independence of working at my own pace, using the *Reader's Guide to Periodical Literature*, filling out note cards, and putting them together into an understandable paper. I got an A on both papers.

More importantly, the research skills I learned from Mrs. Schilling helped me through my entire academic career. I knew I could count on a minimum grade of B+ on any college term paper that I wrote, and most often I got an A. In fact, by the time I hit graduate school, I got As on all my research papers.

In the late 1960s, at a Newell High School reunion of all classes I had a chance to thank Mrs. Schilling and Mrs. George for the tremendous amount of hard work and caring they had put into their teaching. I hope that a thanks was some reward for their perseverance and the respect for education they showed.

After a rocky start in high school, my high ACT score and my improved academic performance during my junior and senior years seemed to signal that I would be capable of doing college work. I narrowed my choices to West Virginia University in Morgantown, where I had been to a number of football games, and West Liberty State College, a small teachers' college located in the hills back of Wheeling, and only a one-hour drive from home. I had friends attending each school and classmates who were planning to attend each the next fall.

I did not think that acceptance to a West Virginia college would be a problem because the admission rule in West Virginia at that time was that state colleges and universities were required to accept any graduate of a West Virginia high school who graduated in the top three-quarters of their class. I applied to both colleges and even applied for a scholarship at West Liberty, despite having only a 2.0 GPA at the end of my junior year. Dad drove me to West Liberty on a cold, rainy Saturday morning in March during my senior year to take the scholarship tests and to have an interview with Dr. Bartell, the Dean of Men and a former football coach.

To my surprise I was wait-listed at West Virginia University, which meant that the admission decision would be held until I actually graduated from high school. Bill Moffitt, Joe May, Denise Bowen, and Sue Ellen Logston were all granted early admission to WVU. As March dragged into April, I weighed my options. West Liberty was closer to home and smaller, so I could get more personal attention. On the other hand, WVU carried more prestige because it was the state university and they played major college football and basketball, which I was interested in watching.

As time wore on more of my friends were making their college choices. Larry Hutton decided to attend the University of Cincinnati in the engineering co-op program, Mary Nease opted for Fairmont State College, and Tom Woods chose Potomac State Junior College in Keyser, West Virginia. Bill Moffitt, Joe May, and Denise Bowen were headed for West Virginia University. My girlfriend, Liz Arner, was accepted to Duke University, and my classmates Mary Huff and Ruth McCabe decided on West Liberty State College. I was starting to feel college choice pressure.

Then, on a beautiful sunny afternoon in early May, Mr. Seevers, the mailman brought the fateful letter. The thin letter on West Liberty State College stationery was from the Office of the President. My hands actually trembled as I slowly opened the envelope that could hold my future in its contents. I had to read only the first sentence to know where I would be going to college. "Congratulations," it read, "you have been awarded a West Virginia Board of Education Tuition Waiver to attend West Liberty State College." Apparently my ability to take standardized tests had trumped my low high school grades and my tuition would be waived for four years as long as I remained a student in good standing. Tuition was $100 a semester then, and room and board at West Liberty ran $600 a year, so the tuition waiver represented about 24% of the cost of college. The money was significant, and more than that, West Liberty not only accepted me but really seemed to want me. The scholarship also reinforced my small grain of confidence that I could go to college, make the grades, graduate and everything would work out for the best.

The next fall I was wearing the black and orange freshman beanie of West Liberty State in a student body of 1,400, the highest enrollment in the history of the school to that date. I was happy to be there.

⌐

The Newell High School class of 1961 produced a number of college graduates and other alumni who have had successful careers. Sue Ellen Logston Fox earned a J.D. and I received a Ph.D. Bill Moffitt and Larry Hutton received business degrees, and Joe May earned an electrical engineering degree from West Virginia

University. Denise Bowen May (West Virginia University), Mary Nease Brandal (Fairmont State College), and Ruth McCabe Fuller (West Liberty State) all received teaching degrees. Margaret Donovan Porton earned a master's degree in counseling (Duquesne University) and Frank Gilmore received a degree in business (University of Missouri—St. Louis). We have gone on to successful careers in business and education. Other members of the class also had successful careers; Ron Noland in criminal justice, Joe Fuller as a teamster, Eugene Hart in industry, Dixie Miller Lee in cosmetic sales, and Jim Haynes in the ministry like his father. I am sure that other classmates were equally successful, although I have lost track of them. We really had a smart class and the Newell education system worked well for us.

Besides learning how to write term papers, we also learned to respect education. We never felt our teachers were just going through the motions; we knew they believed in the importance of education and we should also.

Newell High School also gave me the self-confidence that comes from performing in front of people. Small high schools provide a greater opportunity for the students to shine. I not only caught touchdown passes in football games, but I also read the prayer at commencement, decorated for the prom, refereed girls' basketball games, and attended formal dances. This was done not in front of strangers but in front of people who mattered, Newell people who had known me all my life. More than a shoe shine and a smile, these were the things that gave me the confidence to take bigger steps in life.

Some of the Newell Volunteer Fire Department pose with Truck Number One. The firemen put on the Firemen's Carnival annually in the 1950s. (Photo from the 1957 Newell High School Yearbook)

Chapter 6

My Brother Was a Carny

During the school year the high school sports and the high school activities provided most of the entertainment in Newell. But in the summer when school was not in session and things got pretty quiet, the absolute high point of the social season was the Firemen's Carnival.

The Fireman's Carnival lasted for a week in July, usually beginning just when heat, humidity, and boredom began to become oppressive. The carnival, a fundraiser for the Newell Volunteer Fire Department and other service clubs, had something for everyone—a parade, a brightly lit midway, gambling, food, carnival rides, and, of course, bingo. For one glorious week each summer the Newell firemen transformed the left and center field sections of Clarke Field into a magical land. The Newell Carnival did not rival what went on in Rio de Janeiro or even the carnivals in Weirton or Follansbee, but it provided a definite bright spot in an otherwise uneventful summer.

The Fireman's Carnival varied little from year to year, but replaying the ritual each year with a slightly different cast of characters was part of the point. It was a little like watching *Oklahoma* after you had seen the movie and the play performed three or four times. Watching something that you know inside out and love to see is comforting, but it is also interesting to see how that performance will vary with different actors and actresses. The sameness of the Fireman's Carnival from year to year was reassuring, because it meant that the world would not change too quickly and that the familiar patterns of life would go on.

The Newell Volunteer Fire Department was founded in 1907. Because it was a volunteer company in an unincorporated town, the firemen had to raise all their own funds. Their major fundraising projects were the annual carnival and weekly bingo games. The firemen were so successful at raising money that they were able to buy two new fire trucks and build a new, brick fire station in the 1950s. In addition to housing the fire trucks and firefighting equipment, the new firehouse had a large room in the back that was big enough to hold weekly bingo games and was rented out for spaghetti dinners, dances, and wedding receptions.

There were about twenty-five Newell volunteer firemen, mostly young guys in their twenties or thirties who were factory workers at Homer Laughlin, Edwin M. Knowles, Globe Brick, or one of the steel mills in the area. They were the kind of guys who liked the adventure of fighting fires or riding on fire trucks in parades. They also seemed to like getting out of the house in the evening and hanging out at the firehouse. In nice weather they sat in front of the firehouse on folding chairs leaned up against the building, and drank Nehi orange soda or Coca-Cola and told jokes and stories. They seemed like a comfortable fraternity, at ease in each other's company, yet ready to leap into action and speed away on their trucks the minute the fire siren went off.

The carnival excitement began to grow on Friday evening when the firemen started building their stands and escalated on Sunday when the carnies brought in the rides on battered trucks that looked like they had seen too many miles on rural back roads. The carnival opened on Monday, and closed on the following Saturday night with a grand finale, complete with fireworks. A parade was thrown in sometime during the week. Monday night always drew a big crowd because it was opening night and gave people a chance to size up the new edition of the carnival, but mostly it was a chance to get out in the cool evening air after a hot summer day and socialize with people from the community.

The most spectacular Newell Firemen's Carnival ever was held in 1957, the summer before my freshman year. Newell held a Golden Jubilee celebration to observe the fifty-year anniversary of the founding of the town, even though Newell was never incorporated. The carnival was the culmination of the celebration, and the firemen vowed to put on a big show even if they did not make money on the carnival. So they socked big bucks into the parade, hired a high-wire act to perform at 9:00 each night, and sponsored a huge fireworks display for Saturday, the final night of the Golden Jubilee celebration.

The parade was like any other small-town parade, only smaller. The parade route was ten blocks long, and that included winding through town twice. The parade units lined up at Sixth and Grant streets and proceeded down Grant to Second Street, where the parade made a right turn and marched on to Washington, the town's main street, where it made another right turn and then traveled five blocks back to the carnival grounds on Clarke Field.

In 1957 the parade was on Saturday night. Scheduled to begin at 7:00, it would pass in front of our house at 308 Grant Street. At 7:00 sharp Mom and Dad were sitting on the porch to watch, but my sister Janie and I stationed ourselves right beside the street so we could get a close view of everything. The fireman offered so much prize money that the parade was larger than usual with thirty units. The start of the parade was delayed thirty-five minutes

My sister Janie, on the front porch of our house at 308 Grant Street. The fireman's parade route ran right in front of our house.

because it took so long to get all of the units in place. The Hancock County Sheriff's car, driven that year by Sheriff Clayton B. Hobbs, always led the parade; ironically, that was one of the few times I ever saw the Hancock County sheriff's car in Newell even though he and his deputies were our only law enforcement officers since we had no police force.

Though a small parade, it was ours, going down the street right in front of our house. There were only two high school marching bands, but the bands' uniforms added a splash of color. Besides the green and white marching band from Newell High School, that year the parade drew the purple and gold band from our rival, Chester High School. Each band played its fight song, stolen (as I found out later) from college fight songs. The Newell fight song used the words and tune from West Virginia University's fight song, "It's West Virginia." The Chester band used the Indiana University fight song.

Since Newell was small and unincorporated, we did not have any city officials, so there were fewer politicians than in most parades. We had trouble even attracting important people like the Hancock County commissioners and instead had to settle for justices of the peace. Because Chester was a bigger city, the Chester parade that year drew West Virginia's Republican Governor Cecil Underwood and Republican Congressman Arch Moore, and Chester's Republican mayor, George Scott (my future wife's uncle).

But, the Newell parade had royalty. Brenda Staley the queen of the Golden Jubilee and sister of my friend Mickey, and her court rode in convertibles, but the real feature in '57 was the fire trucks. There were at least a dozen trucks from as far away as Weirton, West Virginia, and Slovan and Midland, Pennsylvania, which were twenty-five and thirty-five miles away. The new $32,000 fire truck from Midland won the $50 first prize for best fire truck. The sounds of the fire sirens mixed with the marching band music were deafening up close, but cranked up our adrenaline and were a big part of the excitement of a parade.

The Newell High School Big Green marching band and the Newell fire truck had the place of honor at the end of the parade. I looked for my classmates Larry Hutton, Mary Huff, and Sue Ellen Logston, who were in the band, and Sharon Haddox, the prettiest girl in our class, who had just become a majorette. She looked stunning in her little puffy majorette hat, short green skirt, and the cowgirl boots that all majorettes wore. I yelled and waved to them and they smiled, but couldn't turn their heads while they

The 1956 - 57 Newell High School Big Green Marching Band. (Photo from the 1957 Newell High School Yearbook)

were marching. After the parade passed our house, Janie and I ran around the corner to again watch the parade march down Washington Street in the other direction. The *East Liverpool Review* estimated that 2,000 people lined the streets of Newell to watch the parade. Some may have been counted twice.

Following the parade the carnival grounds were filled with visiting firemen, many of whom stopped in one of Newell's bars for a shot and a beer, the standard drink for factory workers and coal miners of that era, before they headed home.

Although it was called the Fireman's Carnival, the fair was really a fundraising enterprise for the whole town. The Women's Club always had a booth. Ever since it began in 1937, belonging to the Woman's Club was the stamp of respectability and prestige that every young woman from twenty to forty longed for. My mom was thrilled when she was invited to join soon after we moved to Newell and belonged to the club the entire time we lived there.

The Newell Women's Club in 1957. My mom, Helen Barnett, is the second from the right in the first row. (Photo from the 1957 Newell High School Yearbook)

The Fireman's Carnival gave the members a chance to show off in a tasteful way. They had a bake sale every year. They knew their market well because in the 1950s my family and every other family I knew had dessert every night. Mom always got to the carnival early to buy the best desserts before the booth opened to the public. The other club members did the same and most of the baked goods were gone by the time the booth opened. The club sold out of everything before 8:00 each night. It was always a successful fundraiser enabling the club to give a $100 scholarship to a Newell High School senior, to sponsor the annual dinner dance for the senior class and to buy playground equipment.

For men in Newell, belonging to the Lion's Club, marked them as the civic leaders of the town. Men like Coach John Robison and Albert Logston, the father of my friend Sue Ellen, who was a foreman in the pottery and a charter member of the club, were typical of the grocers, teachers, salesmen, and supervisors in the brick yard or pottery who belonged to the club. My dad was president of the club in 1960 - 61, his greatest achievement in Newell. The Lion's Club always sponsored the dart throw. A dime bought you three darts to throw at balloons tacked to a corkboard. Breaking one balloon won a candy bar and breaking three balloons won a box of twenty-four candy bars.

Other organizations such as the American Legion, the Band Boosters, and Athletic Boosters had stands that changed each year. Nevertheless, I could count on some group sponsoring a booth where I could try to throw ping-pong balls into goldfish bowls to win a live goldfish. My ping pong balls inevitably bounced away, but my brother Jimbo once won a goldfish. He carried it home carefully in a baggie filled with water. It lived for two weeks. I had better luck at the booth where I tossed nickels into glass bowls. I won a candy dish which I took home to Mom. She used it for years.

The centerpiece of the carnival was the firemen's bingo. Primarily a woman's game, bingo drew fifty or sixty fanatical females who played from 7:00 p.m. straight through to 11:00. This was my mom's favorite carnival activity. She spent hours each night putting down two nickels for two cards in game after game, hoping to go BINGO and win the jackpot, three to five dollars, depending on how many people were playing. Coupled with the music from the merry-go-round, the sound of the bingo caller on the loudspeaker created a wall of sound throughout the grounds.

Although women flocked to the bingo tables, the most popular games for men and boys involved gambling. Boys learned to gamble at an early age in Newell and no one seemed to object. If a boy was

The Newell Lions club in 1957. My father, Clarence Barnett, is the third person from the left in the front row. Coach Robison is the tall guy in the middle back row. (Photo from the 1957 Newell High School Yearbook)

tall enough to put his money on the counter, he was old enough to gamble, at least at the Firemen's Carnival. Even boys who were too short to reach the counter could still play if they got someone taller to place their bets. My personal favorite game was a version of dice baseball run by the Odd Fellows. The Odd Fellows were a semi-secret service club that had a clubhouse on Washington Street next to the Jefferson Elementary School playground. They were so secret that I did not know anything about them except that they ran the dice baseball game. It was played with two large six-sided dice almost the size of softballs. One of the dice had the name of a different baseball team printed on each of its six sides. The other had six numbers printed on its sides. After we had placed our bets of anything from a nickel to a dollar on the name of a team painted on the three-sided booth's counter, the Odd Fellow who ran the game rolled the dice down a slanted chute. When the dice stopped rolling, the team name on the top side of the dice won, with the payoff determined by the number on the second dice. Potentially the payoff could be six times the bet. However, it does not take a mathematical genius to understand that the odds of winning are six to one, but the payoff will be less than six to one on five of the six possible outcomes. Anyone who played for long was sure to lose money. Unfortunately, I was not a mathematical genius. I lost a lot of hard-earned nickels at the dice baseball game because, like all gamblers, I believed I would be lucky enough to beat the odds. The Firemen's Carnival was the place I learned that gambling is where you give someone your money and they keep it.

The rides at the carnival were small-time even by Newell standards. A company brought in four or five children's rides— little boats and cars, spinning tea cups, and a tired looking merry-go-round with horses that looked like they should be put out to pasture. The only adult ride was a Ferris wheel. Every junior high boy recognized the opportunity the Ferris wheel held. Here was a chance to be alone with a girl and even though the lights were bright, there was the possibility of holding hands. For girls, the carnival was where you found out who you were going to date the rest of the summer, recalled Susie McKenna Bebout (class of 1962) at a recent Newell High School reunion.

During the 1957 carnival I asked Susan Tucker, a girl I had been interested in off and on for a couple of years, to ride on the Ferris wheel. Asking her wasn't hard. Everyone already knew that I was interested in her since I had asked her to go to a dance with me at the end of the school year. But once alone with her on the Ferris wheel, I was too shy to try to hold her hand. The ride wasn't a complete loss; the view from the top of the wheel was interesting. I thought that I would be able to see for miles, but I was really only able to see the rooftops of the houses in the lower end of Newell and the rooftop of the high school.

The ride operators were the only real carnies at the Newell Carnival, and they were a sorry lot. I knew what carnies should be like because my Grandmother Hulda had read *Toby Tyler, or Ten Weeks With the Circus* to me when I was five-years old. The book is a cautionary tale in which Toby, a young boy in a small town, is lured into running away to join what he believes will be an exciting life with the circus. He learns the circus is hard work and from the circus grounds looking out, one town is pretty much the same as any other. After ten weeks he runs away from the circus, and after an arduous journey he arrives at home where he begs to be forgiven and permitted to live with his family again. After hearing about Toby, I was not tempted to join the carnies, but I hoped they would be interesting—loud, wild, lusty, drunken, tattooed guys who said funny things to get people to ride on the rides. But these carnies didn't hype the rides, chase local girls, get drunk in local bars, or even try to lure local boys into running away to join the circus. They did not seem to have enough energy to be interesting. They were such nonentities they made staying at home in Newell seem a lot more exciting than running away with them to join the carnival.

My brother Jim did become a carny. His career started when he was going into third grade, shortly after he had changed his name from Jimmy to Jimbo. He missed dinner one evening during carnival week and that was alarming. Jimbo never missed a meal. Mom was worried because she hadn't seen him since lunch, but we all had an idea where he was. Jimbo was a huge fan of the Fireman's Carnival and spent most of his time there during carnival week. After dinner, Dad went directly to the carnival, and sure enough, he found Jimbo helping the firemen get set up for the evening. The firemen had picked him to be one of their junior volunteers, who would run errands and generally help out with the carnival. This was a

My brother Jimbo, now known as Jim, about the time he was a carny.

high honor for Jimbo because he loved the carnival. As a reward for their work, Jimbo and the other volunteers were allowed to stay on the carnival grounds for the week and to camp out with the night crew, who guarded the carnival grounds. Jimbo was essentially gone for the whole week; the only time we saw him was when he came home a couple of times to change clothes and, of course, when we went to the carnival.

A week at the carnival sounded like high adventure to me. Camping on the carnival grounds with the firemen conjured up visions of running through the town at 2:00 a.m., watching the firemen drink beer and listening to outrageous stories about firemen adventures with wild women or at least about fighting fires. But according to Jimbo it was pretty tame. The carnival closed for the night around 11:00. After a short cleanup the crew of six or eight men sat around a small campfire, roasted marshmallows, and then went to bed on cots in a big tent. They got up early in the morning. The men finished the cleanup and the kids combed the carnival grounds for money that people had dropped the previous night. Jimbo and the other kids often picked up a dollar or more if they had sharp eyes.

I recently asked Jim (he became Jim after our family moved to Columbus in 1963) what he remembered from his life as a carnie. "They put too much pepper on the eggs in the morning," was his reply. I pumped him for more information, but he did not have anything else to say. Was this a failure of memory on his part? Or maybe there was a Firemen's Carnival code of silence similar to the Las Vegas code: "What happens on the carnival grounds at night stays on the carnival grounds."

The food at the Newell Firemen's Carnival was typical of most carnivals. They served hot dogs, popcorn, candy, and those carnival standards, cotton candy and candy apples. But the firemen did sell one food that was spectacular, a treat of such gourmet proportions that it will forever live in the minds of Newell carnival goers. The Fireman's Carnival fish sandwiches were food for the gods.

I am not sure why those fish sandwiches were so delicious. They consisted of frozen whitefish coated with bread crumbs and were deep fried. Gene Lytton who joined the Newell Volunteer Fire Department in 1957 and still goes out to fight fires at age seventy-seven said that the fish was so good because they changed the grease frequently. The firemen set up at least a dozen home-style Honeywell Deep Fryers, the kind with the picture of the chef on the end. The chef's eyes light up red when the grease is hot enough to cook. An assembly line of firemen dumped the steaming fish from the deep fryers into a pan lined with paper towels. Just as quickly, with the steam still rising and smelling of hot grease, the fish were put on white bread buns and served to a long line of waiting customers. There was no fancy tartar sauce. Everyone doused the fish with catsup and wolfed the sandwiches down; sometimes the fish was so hot it burned your tongue. The delectable taste of hot fish, greasy bread crumbs, on a soft bun, and dripping catsup spoke to our taste buds as nothing else had ever done before. From every mouthful of fish came the same moan of high praise, "It doesn't taste fishy." Actually it did not taste like anything I had ever eaten before. From Monday when the carnival opened until the last light was turned out on Saturday, those Honeywell fryers worked at full steam to produce that rare delicacy, but they barely could keep up with the demand.

My friend Marilyn Gibas contended the fish sandwiches were good because we had them only once a year. However, she later confessed to having fish sandwiches every Friday at St. Aloysius Elementary School, the Catholic grade school in East Liverpool. "But they were not anything like the carnival fish sandwiches," she said. "My family didn't eat meat on Friday because we were Catholic, but we did not have fish because my father didn't like fish. He did like the fish sandwiches from the Firemen's Carnival," she added with a wry smile.

No one in my immediate or extended family liked eating or catching fish, and while some of my friends fished I don't remember any of them eating the fish they caught. One reason for the lack of interest in fishing was concern about water pollution from human and industrial wastes. Even though we lived on the Ohio River in the 1950s no one ate any of the numerous carp or catfish caught there because we believed the fish were contaminated by swimming in polluted waters.

My mom, who was a good cook, did serve fish at least once every other week on Friday (even though we were not Catholic), because it was an inexpensive meal. However, she didn't like to eat fish, she didn't like the smell, and she didn't know how to prepare it. She always bought some kind of a grey-looking frozen fish that came in square packages and when defrosted fell into strange shapes that did not resemble anything I had ever seen before or since. That was before Mrs. Paul's Fish Sticks. The breading always fell off when Mom tried to pan fry the fish. The fish looked even grayer after frying with no bread crumbs to hide behind. The grey fish had a soggy texture and a strong ammonia taste which we associated with a fishy taste, but which I suspect had more to do with poor freezing. Lots of catsup made this mess only barely edible.

In the mid-1950s my family made a major purchase: a Honeywell Deep Fryer, just like the firemen used. We expected fish sandwiches like the carnival's would immerge. But even with the Honeywell Mom could not master fish. The batter still fell off, and the fish became even greyer, greasier, and tougher to chew. The deep fryer was not a complete loss. My mom became a master at making French fries (cooking secret—use long white potatoes, soak the cut-up fries in ice cold water for an hour before cooking, and while cooking, poke the potatoes periodically with a meat fork to help them soak up more grease) with that Honeywell.

Fish sandwiches became so popular in Newell that the Newell Civic Council, the group that took over the annual carnival from the firemen and renamed it the Festival of Clay, later built a permanent building on Clarke Field so that they could serve fish sandwiches year round on Fridays, Saturdays, during flea markets, and of course during the Festival of Clay. Not to be outdone, the Lions Club of Newell purchased a building on Washington Street where they cook and sell fish sandwiches on Fridays. "We don't cook fish during the summer because there just isn't enough business, but the rest of the year we do really well," said Lions Club member Marilyn Gibas. "Most of our business is lunch deliveries to the plants in the area or carryout dinners. We cook frozen, already breaded fish and serve them on sub buns. We get them from the same place the Civic Council gets their fish. The fish sandwiches that we cook are really good, but not as good as the fish sandwiches from the Firemen's Carnival." But then nothing since has ever been that good.

The 1953 Chester Legion Giants Little League Baseball Team. I am second from the left in the first row. (Photo courtesy of Susan Miller Panebianco)

Chapter 7

Tickets to the Series

～

I dreamed of playing major league baseball when I was growing up. But then so did every other boy in mid-century America. The post-World War II period was baseball's second golden age, second only to the Babe Ruth era in the 1920s. Fans turned out in record numbers to watch major league games. The rest of us listened to the games on sultry summer days on Philco radios as we lay on gliders on front porches. Baseball was America's game.

Newell was a baseball town. The 1948 Newell High School baseball team advanced all the way to the semifinal game of the state tournament, where they lost 3 - 2 to Williamson High School, the eventual state champions. That was an amazing feat because the state had only one classification in baseball and Newell, one of the smallest high schools in the state with a baseball team, had to beat a number of larger high schools to get to the semifinal game.

Newell players went away to small, minor-league cities hoping to realize their dreams of eventually making the big leagues. Six players from Newell had minor-league baseball careers in the 1940s, the best of whom was Stan Franczek, a third baseman who was signed by the St. Louis Cardinals organization and started his professional career with Johnson City, Tennessee in the Appalachian League. Franczek advanced to the Class A level team in Fresno, California before he quit playing in the early 1950s to return to Newell to sell cars for Litten Motors and to raise his family. No one from Newell ever reached the major leagues, not even for a "cup of coffee."

In the late 1940s and the 1950s those men who had gone away for a summer or two to chase their dreams on dusty minor-league ball fields returned to Newell to play for The Homer Laughlin China Company team in the East Liverpool City League. Other league teams included the Irish Town Meat Packers, Golden Star Dairy, and the Midland, Pennsylvania CIO Steelworkers. The City League teams were made up of men back from the war and former high school players who wanted to continue playing baseball for at least another year or two.

The Homer Laughlin team was made up completely of players from Newell, most of whom worked in the pottery, but some held jobs in steel mills or selling insurance. They played in front of crowds of up to 200 spectators on pleasant summer evenings in the pre-television era. I was eight- and nine-years old when the City League was at its zenith, and the home games of the Homer Laughlin team were played just half a block from my house, at Clarke Field.

I went to every home game to watch, and I eventually became part of the team. At every game during the summer when I was nine, I was either a batboy or a foul ball chaser. Both were great jobs, but chasing balls paid money. The two kids who chased balls were paid, as was the umpire, with money collected from passing a hat through the grandstand. We earned as much as a dime for every foul ball retrieved from foul territory and returned to the umpire. One chaser was stationed on each side of the field, so if a foul ball was hit down the left field line the chaser on that side of the field took off running to get the ball. Foul balls hit straight back and over the screen were fair game for either chaser. On my best day ever I chased down seven foul balls and got fifty cents after the game. But even on my worst days I would get at least three foul balls and collect twenty-five cents minimum. Unfortunately for me ball chasing usually went to bigger, faster kids, so I most often got to be batboy.

The batboy's job was to keep the bats lined up parallel to each other on the ground near the bench so that the players could easily find their bats when they went to the on-deck circle. When the batter hit the ball and ran to first base, the batboy had to run up to the plate and retrieve the bat. Almost all of the batboy's work was done when his team was at bat. When his team was in the field, there was not much to do except run an occasional errand for the manager or one of the players on the bench. I loved being a batboy because I felt that I was part of the game, and I got my choice of any two of the bats that were broken during the game. All teams played with wooden bats in those days, and three or four bats might be broken during a game. Usually the bats were only cracked and could be repaired and used in pickup games. As a result, I always had at least five or six cracked bats in my collection of baseball equipment. Unfortunately they were man-sized bats, ranging from thirty-three to thirty-six inches, much larger than the Little League bats that were twenty-nine to thirty-two inches. When I used the bats in pick-up games I was forced to choke up on the bat, and even then it was hard to get a level swing.

The sweetest time to play baseball in Newell was in the very early spring. In 1953, when I was in fourth grade, the first true spring day occurred in Newell in late March, following a mild spell which had melted the last pile of dirty slush but hadn't yet greened the grass. The morning sun rose unusually bright. The ground was damp, but not muddy. It was warm enough that my mom didn't force me to wear boots, my winter coat, or my hat with earflaps. Instead, she took my tennis shoes, sweatshirt, spring jacket, and baseball cap, all faintly smelling of mothballs, from the closet and chest of drawers. Clearly, it was a day for the first baseball game of the year.

I found my baseball glove in the back of the downstairs closet buried under a mound of boots, snow pants, and a stray winter coat or two. It was just as it had been left in the autumn, with the four large rubber bands still wrapping it around a baseball to make a pocket. The ball had turned a little brown from the neat's-foot oil I had smeared on the glove to keep it soft over the winter.

My favorite baseball bat, a beautiful, thirty-five-inch, thick-handled Jackie Robinson model, leaned in the other corner of the closet. I had carefully selected it from the broken bat pile at one of the Homer Laughlin games and lovingly repaired it with tiny screws, tacks, and electrical tape until it was almost as good as new. Unfortunately, my official Pittsburgh Pirates baseball cap didn't survive as well as the other equipment. Somehow it had been put into the toy box and had spent the winter being crushed. The bill that I had so carefully molded into an inverted U now looked more like a lopsided S. But at least it still fit.

The run to the field was an invigorating experience. The tennis shoes felt like part of my feet, my arms and legs moved freely, and the wind whistled past my ears, which had for too many months been protected by earflaps.

As always, choosing teams was a major undertaking because of the disparity of talent which could upset the delicate competitive balance of the teams. If one team took Stinky (last names are not used here for obvious reasons), who did not smell any worse than the rest of us, they would also get the kid who had the pristine white baseball bat, and official Wilson big-league glove, and was the only boy in town with braces. He would not let us use his equipment unless we let him play. But would a team fielding both a kid with braces and a "Stinky" be at too great a psychological disadvantage? If one team took the big eighth grader, they would also have to take the inevitable little brother someone's mother had forced him to bring, the kid who could barely lift a bat and who cried each time he struck out. Fortunately, that is where I learned how to negotiate, a skill that would stand me in good stead the rest of my life. With the tact of a seasoned diplomat and the decisiveness and authority of a hard-nosed negotiator, I proclaimed, "You take Stinky and tinsel mouth. Give us Fat Boy and Bear, and we'll take the little kid."

"Don't call me Stinky," said Stinky. But the matter was settled. A balance of power had been achieved. The game began.

Later, more kids arrived and were absorbed into the game, either by negotiation or by choosing teams again. When there were seven on a side, right field was no longer an automatic out. More kids arrived and replaced the kids whose mothers had called them to lunch.

After lunch the men came to play. Big men. Old men. Some of them juniors and seniors in high school, some of them out of high school and married with little kids of their own. The little brothers, who had cried only three times, and one of whom had actually hit the ball (but in his excitement ran to third base instead of first), were crowded off the field and wandered off to play little kid games. The men took over the infield positions, and the original players moved to the outfield (or maybe second base). That was okay, because the men could throw and hit hard. The ground balls hit by the men made an ugly zinging sound that occasionally meant a bad hop to the face. It was better to be in the outfield than to have everyone see you turn your head on a ground ball I reasoned to myself as I stood in center field.

The men tired quickly. After only a couple of hours, they

had had their fill of baseball for the summer and drifted off to do whatever old men did in the spring. The game dwindled back to seven on a side and then to five. By this time, the game had reached the forty-seven[th] inning or maybe the third inning of the ninth game and no one, not even the weak-hitting and weak-armed *A* student, could remember the score. No one really cared.

Near suppertime, the game began to disintegrate. A sharp line drive was hit between Bob Shenton in left field and Mickey Staley in center field. Neither chased it but instead argued about who should have caught it. Meanwhile, the batter walked around the bases. The next batter hit a grounder to Ronnie Noland, the shortstop. The throw to first was a little low and Larry Hutton, the first baseman, refused either to reach down and scoop it up or to chase it. Suddenly, we were all very tired and hungry. We remembered that our mothers had told us to be home early for dinner. The game was over. Spring had officially sprung in Newell.

Baseball in Newell and in the United States changed very quickly in the 1950s. One of the reasons for the change was the introduction of Little League baseball. I had seen newsreels about Little League baseball in 1950 and thought that it was really neat for kids to get to play on small fields in real baseball uniforms. The next year I watched Follansbee inaugurate its Little League program with a parade of the players from its downtown to the field followed by a series of two-inning games. I could not wait to have a chance to play on a Little League team.

Fortunately East Liverpool, Ohio got caught up in the wave of interest in Little League baseball and started a league the very next year that also included kids from Newell and Chester. The tryouts for places on the teams were held in the spring of 1952. I had just turned nine so I was old enough to play. I went with some of the other kids from the lower end of Newell to Vodrey Field in East Liverpool to try out for one of the four teams in the new league.

When we got there I was shocked. The field was crowded with hundreds of other kids between the ages of nine and twelve. All of them were bigger than me. The coaches gave each of us a number printed on cardboard to be pinned to the back of our shirt. Then we got in huge lines where we had to show how well we could throw, catch, and field ground balls. Because my glove was an old first baseman's mitt, the top of it flopped down when I tried to open it to catch the ball. I had to chase a lot of balls that I missed because of that glove. When the coaches drafted their teams I was not picked to even try out for one of the four teams. I had not impressed any of the coaches enough to be given a chance.

That summer, when I was visiting my grandmother in Follansbee, I tried my friend Johnny Bates' glove. It was rich, brown leather, a Wilson brand, Eddie Mathews model. A fielder's glove, it was designed with three fingers instead of four so that its pocket was just between my thumb and forefinger and just below the large web. To my surprise, I could catch the ball easily and all of a sudden I was a much better player. Johnny told me that the glove cost six dollars at the hardware store.

I knew that my parents would not buy me that glove; they felt the one I had was perfectly good, and six dollars was a lot of money then. So I went to my Uncle Dick, my favorite uncle. He was effervescent and, as the youngest of nine brothers and sisters, was still a big kid himself even though he was in his twenties. Uncle Dick was not married at the time and, with no children of his own, lavished affection on his nephews and nieces. Not only that, but he was extremely interested in sports. When I explained my problem, Uncle Dick understood, since his family had never had much money for extras when he was growing up. When he said that he would pay for half of the new glove if I could get the money to pay for the other half, I was thrilled. That afternoon I begged a dollar each from Grandma Hulda, Aunt Norma, and Aunt Ada to get my three dollars.

The next morning Uncle Dick took me to the hardware store. I was surprised to see the glove actually cost $7.50, instead of the $6.00 that I had been told. Now my three dollars was not half the price. Uncle Dick looked at me holding the glove and asked the clerk for a marking pen. He crossed out the $7.50 on the box and marked in $6.00 and paid the clerk $7.50. He made one little boy very happy.

That glove was so good that it practically caught the ball by itself. I practiced as much as I could all that summer until football season when I carefully rubbed the glove with neat's-foot oil, put a ball in the pocket, creased the glove in just the right place, and carefully put it away with large rubber bands holding it closed with the ball in the pocket.

Undaunted, and now ten, I tried out for the Little League again in the spring of 1953. I wanted to be picked by The Homer Laughlin China Company Pirates, a team that practiced and played most of its games in Newell. Instead, I was picked to play on the Chester American Legion Giants, a team with a majority of players from Chester that practiced in Chester about a mile from my home. But I was just happy to have a team tryout.

After two weeks of preseason practice I survived the final team cuts and received my uniform. It was grey with the words Chester American Legion across the front in orange, a blue and white Little League patch on the right sleeve and an orange number on the back. The cap and long baseball socks were in royal blue. The uniform numbers corresponded with the size of the uniform. Mark Bulger, a giant ten-year-old, got number 15. I was given number 1 because I was the smallest player on the team, but I was ecstatic. That was my first official baseball uniform. I wore it for the rest of the day, even that evening when we made the half-hour trip to Weirton to visit Uncle Jim, Aunt Bess, and my cousins Cindy and Margaret Anne. Uncle Jim proudly took a picture of me in my uniform with his Polaroid camera.

Ironically, our opponent for the first game of the season was The Homer Laughlin China Company Pirates. I knew most of their players because they were from Newell and we had played pickup games with each other for the past couple of years.

I did not start the game, but instead sat on the bench. At that time, there was no rule that everyone had to play, but when we had a two-run lead in the last of the sixth inning I was sent in to play left field. The Pirates rallied in their last at bat and put runners on first and second base, and with one out Deuce Dunlevy, their cleanup hitter, came to bat. At five-feet, eight-inches he was big for a Little League player, and was more than a foot taller than me. He dominated pickup games in Newell even when older kids played. Because he hit left-handed, I didn't think there was much chance that he would hit the ball to me in left field. I played at the normal depth that I played for a right-handed hitter, and a little off the left field line.

I was wrong. Deuce blasted a first pitch fastball deep into the left field corner. I turned to my right and ran as fast as I could. After running for miles, it seemed, at the last second I made a desperate grab for the ball near the fence. I looked in my glove. I looked again. I was astounded to see the ball stuck in the web. I had, by some miracle, actually caught the ball. With adrenaline flowing, I ripped the ball from the web and fired it to second base, almost doubling the runner off second. We got the next batter to hit into an infield groundout to preserve the win.

My teammates and the coaches pounded me on the back and shook my hand. "Thanks," was all I could think to mumble, but an ear-to-ear smile was on my face. When my parents and I got home and were walking from the garage to our house, one of the neighbors asked us who won. My mom proudly bragged, "We did, and Bobby made a catch that saved the game."

I was thrilled to be a minor hero in my first organized baseball game, but I wasn't surprised. I had always believed I would be a star player. However, over the next two years I found out I was in fact not very good. That catch turned out to be the high point of my Little League career.

During my two years of Little League baseball I played sparingly, mostly because I could not hit. The coach told my mother he thought I was too tired to play because I was playing too many pickup games on game day afternoons. Mom made me come home and rest on game days. I thought, "Why should I rest? So I can be fresh to sit on the bench?"

The summer of 1954 was one of the greatest baseball seasons in the history of the game, at least as far as my friends and I were concerned. Because Newell is in the Northern Panhandle of West Virginia, we were in the listening areas for both the Pittsburgh Pirates and the Cleveland Indians. The Indian games came in over WOHI from East Liverpool across the river. We listened to the Pirate games on KDKA radio from Pittsburgh.

Most people in our area rooted for the Indians because they were winners. But it was only an hour's drive to Pittsburgh and more than three to Cleveland. The logic of an eleven-year-old mind demanded loyalty to the closer town despite the Pirates being the worst team in baseball in the early 1950s. They had only one heady, seventh-place finish in 1951 but otherwise were cellar dwellers from 1950 through 1955. It was tough to get excited about the double play combination of Curt Roberts and Gair Allie. But pain, denial, and loyalty were part of life in the 1950s.

The decade belonged to the legendary Yankees: Whitey, Mickey,

Yogi, Billy Martin, Phil Rizzuto, Hank Bauer, Moose Skowron, Bob Grim, Ed Lopat, Allie Reynolds, and seemingly hundreds more. They were power, skill, big city; they were invincible. Eight times in the 1950s they won American League pennants. Meanwhile, the Cleveland Indians served as worthy contenders. Six times during the '50s they finished as American League bridesmaids, five times to the Yankees, but not in 1954.

That was a great time for fans in Newell. The Yankees and Indians battled for the pennant all season. Most of my friends were Indian fans and listened to every game, but there were two or three exceptions that played hide-and-seek after dark with girls. We didn't know why they would want to do that and neither did they; it was just something they were moved to do. Later we understood.

I got caught up in pennant fever. The Pirates were still my team, but it was hard not to get excited about the Indians. Even my coach was captivated. Normally every Little League team in the area got free tickets to Little League Day, usually a Sunday double-header in Cleveland with a loser like the Washington Senators or Philadelphia Athletics. Somehow our coach talked the Chester American Legion into buying tickets for a crucial late season double-header with the Yankees. I would like to say that the Indians won both games, but actually I don't remember who won.

The Indians did keep winning and winning. They won not because they had great players but because their players had great seasons, especially Larry Doby (BA .272 HR 32 RBI 126), Al Rosen (BA .300 HR 22 RBI 102), and Roberto Avila (BA .341 HR 15 RBI 67). Everybody played over their heads but what won it was pitching. They had twenty-game winners in Early Wynn and Bob Lemon. Mike Garcia won nineteen, Art Houterman fifteen, and Bob Feller won thirteen of nineteen starts. Even relief pitcher Don Mossi (who looked ugly on his baseball card) was 6 - 1 with a 1.94 ERA.

When the pennant race was over the Yankees had won 103

games, good enough for first place in most seasons. But the Indians had won an astounding 111 games (with only forty-three losses) to take the flag. They were a good team having a magic season, a team of destiny.

The World Series matched the Indians with the New York Giants, who had beaten the *Boys of Summer* Brooklyn Dodgers by five games but appeared to be nothing spectacular. My friends were overjoyed and predicted an easy series for the "Tribe." I must admit I felt it too.

But the real excitement hit when my Uncle Jim announced he had four box seat tickets to the fourth game of the World Series in Cleveland and asked my dad and me to go with him and my cousin Cindy.

Uncle Jim could always come up with tickets for events in Cleveland. He was in sales at the Weirton Steel Company and had strong ties with the Cleveland steel community. People were always giving him presents—tickets to ball games, watches, blenders, ties, even toys. Christmas was a real bonanza at his house. Uncle Jim was always generous; he gave me my first two watches and about twenty or thirty ties.

He and Cindy picked us up at 6:00 a.m. for the three-hour drive to Cleveland. My cousin was a princess. An eighth grader in 1954, Cindy was a junior version of Doris Day, wholesome, attractive, gracious, and modest. Strangely enough, despite being almost perfect, she was fun to be with. She was also considerate and comforting to have around in awkward situations. You had only to follow her lead to do the right thing. "No, thank you, I don't want another one either," I often repeated.

The 1954 World Series was strange. The Indians were heavily favored, but when Willie Mays made **the** catch of Vic Wertz's almost-sure-RBI-producing hit and journeyman pinch hitter Dusty Rhodes hit a tenth-inning home run to win the first game, it seemed as if the Indians' hearts were broken. Two more pinch hits by Rhodes led to two more Giant victories. Surely, the team who only the week before had been considered as one of the greatest teams ever could win the fourth game and avoid a sweep.

That World Series game was different from the other games I had seen in Cleveland with my Little League team. The huge double-deck Cleveland Stadium was as impressive as always. The Little League usually sat in the far reaches of

My cousin Cindy in ninth grade. She always did the right thing, including giving up the World Series ball so I could have it. (Photo courtesy of Cindy Miller Goad)

the second deck in either deep left or right field, higher than the highest fly ball, and farther than the longest home run from the field. The players seemed small.

But Uncle Jim's box seats were seven rows from the field, right behind the Indian dugout. The box seats gave me a whole different perspective on the game. The players looked huge. The crack of the bat sounded like a rifle shot and the fly balls towered above. Hits that appeared to be going over the fence were caught by the shortstop.

The air was different too. It was warm in the Indian summer October sun, but we felt a chill of fall in the air in the shade or when the wind blew. And there was the acrid smell of burning leaves and the moldy smell of decaying leaves. It was a baseball game played in the middle of football season. The traditional bunting that hung from the stands was in full living color rather than TV or newsreel black and white. There was electricity in the air.

I can't remember who I cheered for or even much about the game except, of course, that Cleveland lost 7 - 4. Near the end of the game, the big event occurred. Wally Westlake, the Indians' right fielder, hit a high pop foul in our direction. With my weak sense of depth I thought it was going into the upper deck. But it hit three or four rows behind us. The next thing I knew my father dived headfirst over the back of our seats and emerged with the ball. A World Series ball! Misplayed by some ham-handed fans, the ball bounced and then rolled under the seat directly behind us, which had been vacated only shortly before for a restroom trip. Fate.

My father passed the ball around and then, to my utter disbelief, offered it to my cousin Cindy to keep. "What?" I hissed in a stage whisper loud enough to be heard in the Giants' dugout, "She's a girl!" This would be sexist now, but it was the 1950s. She looked at me, smiled and said, "No, I don't really want it; give it to Bobby." I almost tore her little finger off taking it from her hand. She smiled anyway. That day, she really was a princess.

The rest of the game and the trip home were a blur. I kept the ball in my tweed sport coat pocket and touched it every so often in the dark car. Things were less complicated then, and stories had happy endings.

⟶

The next year, in 1955 when I was twelve and in my last year to play Little League baseball, I was cut from the Chester American Legion Little League team on the last cut before the season was to start. I was embarrassed to be cut from the team, but otherwise I felt free. I liked not having to go to long, boring practices only to sit on the bench during the games. Pickup games with my friends were much more fun.

In the 1950s the mania for youth baseball did not stop with Little League. The East Liverpool area soon started a PONY League for thirteen- and fourteen-year old boys and a Prep League for fifteen- to seventeen-year-olds. Boys in Newell could play organized baseball from age nine through age seventeen.

The PONY League teams were divided geographically, so my team included thirteen and fourteen-year old boys from both Newell and Chester. The team practiced in Chester again, but there were enough Newell kids trying out that transportation was not a problem. Once again, though, I was cut from the team on the last cut. Feeling a little defeated, I did not try out again for the PONY League when I was fourteen.

The landscape in baseball began to change in the mid 1950s. Television kept fans at home and away from the ballparks and little kids took over the game and pushed adults off the fields. "We went down to talk to the people at the Homer Laughlin about sponsoring us again for the next season and they said they were going to give the money to the kids rather than the adults," said Ed Peters, an excellent infielder for the Homer Laughlin team. "They said they were going to sponsor a Little League team instead of us. Most of us played the next season for other teams in East Liverpool." By the end of the decade not one adult man from Newell was playing on a summer baseball team and the two remaining East Liverpool City League teams had to join the Columbiana County League.

In the spring of 1952 my friend Mickey Staley and I bought our first packs of baseball cards for the new season at Young's Grocery Store. As we sat on the store steps in the warm spring sun, looking at the players' cards and contentedly chewing the large slab of hard, pink bubble gum that came in each pack, Mickey began to cough and sputter. "Gum too strong," I teased. "No!" he exclaimed. "I got gypped. I got Lou Burdette in a Milwaukee Braves minor league card." I had to explain to him he had not been gypped, but that the Boston Braves had moved to Milwaukee over the winter and that he was lucky to get a Lew Burdette card because Burdette was one of the few major league players from West Virginia. He stared at me in disbelief because as far as we knew no major league team ever had changed cities, at least not in the last forty or fifty years. In the next couple of years the St. Louis Browns became the Baltimore Orioles and the Philadelphia Athletics became the Kansas City Athletics. In the late 1950s the Dodgers moved to Los Angeles and the Giants moved to San Francisco. The franchise shifting occurred because of declining attendance at major league games. But to us baseball card collectors, it was as if some kind of sacred trust had been broken and baseball would never be the same.

⟶

I went out for the Newell High School baseball team as a freshman in 1957, but high school baseball in Newell was also in serious decline. Few fans and none of the high school girls attended the games. And if girls were not interested in watching, boys were not interested in playing. Plus, we had terrible uniforms. They looked as if they had been bought in a number of different historic eras. They were mismatched—some were grey, some had stripes, and some were white. But the one thing they all had in common was that they were way too big. They must have been bought when giants played for Newell. The size 32 pants I was given wrapped almost double around my twenty-six-inch waist.

Only twelve players showed up for the first meeting of the team because most of the kids had lost interest in baseball. As a result, I actually got to start some games and played enough to earn my first high school varsity athletic letter.

My first high school varsity letter, baseball 1957.

Earning that varsity letter was one of the very high points of my freshman year. The letters were given out at the Class Day Assembly, on the last day of the school year. The only freshmen to letter that year, in any sport, were Dewey McPherson, Tom Woods and I, on the baseball team. The letter was a kelly green *N* outlined in white, with a baseball over crossed bats embroidered in white on the bottom right-hand corner. I immediately purchased a white V-neck sweater and had Mom sew the letter on the sweater. I proudly wore it every chance I could, including at church camp that summer at Davis and Elkins College where all of my Cousin

Bob Gracey's friends from Weirton asked me how someone as small as I was could win a varsity letter. I just smiled.

That summer I played in the Prep League for the Globe Brick Company team comprised of boys from both Newell and Chester. We played against teams from East Liverpool and Weirton. For part of that season I led the team in hitting with a .360 batting average. I was even hitting better than Deuce Dunlevy, who had been a Little League all-star and was playing his last season of organized sports before joining the Marines. Later in the season my average dropped, but I still ended the year hitting a respectable .290.

I played three more years of high school baseball, but never equaled the success of my Prep League season. The high point of my high school baseball career came in my senior year when a major league baseball scout came to our game with Weirton High School to scout Floyd Shuler, the Weirton shortstop. Not only did I get the only hit for Newell in that game to break up a no-hitter for the Weirton pitcher, John Neiman (who later pitched for West Virginia University). A couple of times I ran to first base to catch overthrows from the infield and hold runners from taking an extra base on an overthrow, an unorthodox move for a catcher. The scout told my father that he liked my hustle and would like to come back to see me when I grew up, but I was already a senior in high school and would never grow much bigger than five-feet eight-inches and 125 pounds.

⌐

Despite being cut from my Little League and PONY league teams and never hitting even .300 in four seasons at a small high school, I thought I was a pretty good baseball player. I planned to try out for the college baseball team my freshman year at West Liberty State College, but I went out for the wrestling and golf teams instead. I was a conference champion in wrestling and made the twelve-member golf team. I never played baseball again.

The 1957 Newell High School Baseball Team. I am in the top row fourth from the left. Tom Woods and Dewey McPherson the other freshmen on the team are to my right. (Photo from the 1957 Newell High School Yearbook)

Another reason for baseball fading away was made clear for me in 1958. I had a cold and was worn out from two-a-day basketball practice so I stayed home to watch the National Football League championship game on December 28. In what proved to be a historic game between the New York Giants and the Baltimore Colts, more than 45 million people watched Alan Ameche, the Colts' fullback, plunge one yard for a touchdown, in sudden-death overtime, to give the Colts a 23 - 17 victory. That game demonstrated to those of us watching that the speed and power of football made it a great television game. The long, drawn out time between pitches and the sporadic action made baseball an excellent radio game. It was clear that day that football was the game of the future and baseball the game of the past.

Television wired Newell to the world. Ruth McCabe poses in the living room in front of her family's 1950s television. (Photo courtesy of Ruth and Joe Fuller)

Chapter 8
A Changing World: Movies and Television

The first time I heard television discussed was in 1949 when I was in first grade. The principal at Jefferson Elementary School in Follansbee was screening my eyes to see if I needed glasses. When I had difficulty seeing the letters, he asked if my family had a television set. The principal explained to Miss Jackson, my first grade teacher, that he believed watching too much television would strain children's eyes, but it would not be a problem because television was just a fad.

In Follansbee, it was reasonable to think television would have limited appeal. The hills around the town blocked the signals and only the families living on top of the hills could watch WDTV from Pittsburgh, which had just gone on the air a short time before in January 1949. Like most of the people in town, we did not have a television, but that was soon to change. Within two years, Follansbee had a community cable system with a large antenna on top of a hill that picked up signals from the former WDTV, now called KDKA, and almost everyone had a television set.

Mrs. Haynes, my third grade teacher in Newell, constantly preached about the power of television to show us history in the making. I did not know what she was talking about. I had seen some television at friends' houses and at Uncle Jim and Aunt Bessie's, but other than the 1952 Sugar Bowl I hadn't seen much history in the making. That changed on January 20, 1953, when the teachers at Jefferson Elementary School told us that if we wanted to watch the inauguration of the new president, Dwight Eisenhower, on television, we could come back to school a couple of minutes late from lunch.

My family did not have a television, but a bunch of kids from the lower end of Newell rode back to school every day after lunch with Sue Ellen Logston's father. We gathered in front of the television at her house at 12:20 to watch the bald, former Army general repeat the oath of office to become President of the United States. The day looked cold and windy in Washington, D.C. and the six of us elementary school kids lying on the Logsdons' floor were entranced by the solemn occasion, the pageantry, and the chance to see history being made. I understood what Mrs. Haynes had been trying to tell us about history, and by 12:45 when we left for school, I had fallen in love with television and the things it brought into our living rooms.

⌣

Later in 1952 during the depths of winter, Dad broke over and bought a used TV from Mom's friends Nedra and Smitter Manson for fifteen dollars. That was a good deal, because new televisions cost anywhere from $180 to $399. Unfortunately, after a couple of months the set, a nineteen-inch table model, broke down and began showing three pictures side-by-side. I watched Sihugo Green and the Duquesne University Dukes thrash another college basketball team three times simultaneously in the same night. We brought in a TV repairman, who had a lot of fancy tubes and equipment, but did not seem to know how to use any of his equipment and could not fix our set. He pronounced it dead. Nedra and Smitter made us take our fifteen dollars back.

Soon after the demise of our first set we bought a twenty-one-inch floor model Stewart and Warner television set. My dad insisted on buying the Stewart and Warner, which was a little known brand, instead of a more popular Philco, RCA or DuMont set, because he said that Stewart and Warner made the tubes used in most other sets. He reasoned if they made the best TV tubes then they must make the best sets. He also claimed we got a good deal on the price. Stewart and Warner might have made good parts, but they were not very good at putting them together into a television, because we had constant repair problems during the three years we owned that set. Dad had outsmarted himself again.

When the Stewart and Warner was on the fritz, which was frequently, we watched a small, portable TV that was a hand-me-down from Uncle Jim and Aunt Bess. The portable TV was fine except that the sound would go off periodically. "His fingerprints were on..." intoned early TV detective Boston Blackie. Then silence while Boston Blackie's lips continued to move as if he were in a silent movie. The only thing that would restore the sound was a solid smack with the palm of the hand on the top of the metal television. We took turns thumping the set. When it was my turn I approached the TV and gave it a sharp open-handed rap on the top. A loud thump rang through the room, but no other sound from the TV. "Hit it a little more to the back," advised Dad from the couch. Another thump filled the room, and was followed by "otherwise he would have been to Chicago by now," explained Boston Blackie, who always wrapped up his show with a tricky explanation of how he caught the bad guy. The sound usually lasted for another twenty or thirty minutes. The TV became addicted to being thumped and eventually had to be thumped every five minutes until that eventful day when a particularly hard thump caused the picture to fade away completely. No amount of thumping, turning the set off and on, or changing the channels could restore either the sound or picture. Dad took it to the TV repair shop in East Liverpool; the repairman opened the back of the set, looked inside and just shook his head. We gave our old friend a decent burial over the edge of the pottery dump.

⌐

At first we could get only one channel in Newell as could most the rest of the United States. The Federal Communications Commission had limited the number of stations while it straightened out some technical problems. In Newell, we got WDTV from Pittsburgh. The station, on the DuMont network, was sponsored by the DuMont Company to encourage people to buy the television sets they were making.

Most of the early television shows came over from radio. *Twenty Questions* was one of my family's early favorite radio-to-television shows. *Twenty Questions* was a quiz show which featured a panel of semi-famous contestants who would try to guess the subject—either animal, vegetable, or mineral—in twenty questions that had to be answered only yes or no. This game was a mainstay of radio, television, and long car trips. When I was six-years old I stumped my parents in the mineral category with the term *Iron Curtain*, which of course they carefully explained to me was not really mineral. *The Arthur Godfrey Show*, a variety show with an ensemble cast, was another show that moved directly from daytime radio, along with the soap operas, to become a staple of daytime television.

My family's all-time favorite early television show was *Your Hit Parade*, a half-hour musical show which had moved from radio to television in 1950. Sponsored by Lucky Strike cigarettes, the show featured the top seven songs of the week counted down from number seven to the week's top hit. Four regular singers, Dorothy Collins, Russell Arms, Snooky Lanson, and Gisele MacKenzie, sang the top songs in production numbers that replicated stage plays. The show aired on Saturday night, and Jimbo and Janie could always talk Mom and Dad into letting us stay up late to see what song would be number one. *Your Hit Parade* left the air after the 1959 season, when teenagers took over the music industry and popularized rock and roll. The *Hit Parade* singers were all big band singers who struggled to sing rock songs, and few adults cared what rock and roll song was number one. I had stopped watching a couple years earlier anyway because I was always out on Saturday nights going to dances.

The most famous and most watched children's show from the single-channel era was *The Howdy Doody Show*. Every kid in my age group loved that show. We could be playing an intense game of freeze tag, but when one kid's mom called him to watch Howdy Doody we all unfroze and ran for home. The show had a variety of characters—some, marionette puppets and some, live actors and actresses. Howdy Doody, a puppet, and Buffalo Bob, a real person, were the stars of the show. Also featured were Clarabelle, a mute clown played by Bob Keeshan, who would later be Captain Kangaroo on his own show, and Chief Thunderthud who invented the word "kowabonga" that would reenter the modern vocabulary in the 1990s by way of *The Simpsons* television show. Another live character on the show was the Native American Princess Summerfall Winterspring, about whom I had erotic fantasies even though I was too young to know what erotic fantasies were; I simply wanted to ride off into the sunset with her on an Indian pony. The show featured old-time silent movie film clips and conflicts between the characters that were often resolved with the puppets hitting each other with sticks "Punch and Judy" style.

The program that best captured the early one-channel era of

television was *The Voice of Firestone*, sponsored by the Firestone Tire and Rubber Company. The program featured opera and classical music. I watched opera, not because I liked it. I actually hated opera, but opera was on the only channel that was available in Newell, and we never turned our set off. The Firestone Company believed that television could spread culture in the United States. I continued to hate opera and believed it was only one step above the test pattern, which I also occasionally watched. Others apparently agreed and some people actually turned their televisions off occasionally because *The Voice of Firestone* had low ratings even with no competition.

The 1940s were the golden age of movies, and all of the kids of my generation grew up as movie fans. One of the real joys of growing up in the 1940s and 1950s was Saturday at the movies. During the dreary days of late winter and early spring when Mom wanted to get me out from underfoot, she gave me thirty-five cents and drove me and a couple of my friends to a kiddie matinee at one of the four theaters in East Liverpool. We could count on an afternoon of pure fun watching a double feature, a serial and a couple of cartoons as well as fifteen minutes of education from the newsreels showing happenings from around the world.

We thought the kiddie matinees would last forever, but by the early 1950s television was making serious inroads into movie attendance. The handwriting was on the wall as early as the winter of 1953. During a visit to Grandma Hulda, I patiently waited in front of the ticket booth of Follansbee's Strand Theater for fifteen minutes on a Saturday afternoon only to be informed by the janitor they were out of the matinee business.

When I was eleven-years old in the spring of 1954, my friends and I attended one of the last great Saturday matinees. Newell was too small to have a theater so we usually went to the movies at one of the four theaters in East Liverpool. Of the four, the American Theater usually showed the best matinees and on this Saturday, it advertised the kiddie matinee to end all kiddie matinees. The matinee featured two movies, *Across the Badlands*, a cowboy movie, and *Rob Roy*, a Walt Disney film about the Scot epic hero. In addition to the feature films and a Three Stooges comedy there were three-color cartoons, including Walt Disney's *Pecos Bill*. "Four solid hours," the ad promised in bold type. This was an event not to be missed. We were easily able to convince our parents to send us when we told them about the four hours.

Four of us went to the show. Mickey Staley was a year younger than me, but so big for his ten years he had to carry a copy of his birth certificate to get in the movie as an under-twelve-year old. Bob Shenton, the oldest, was two-years older than I was and the same size as Mick. The fourth kid of the movie group was Larry Hutton, who was my age and the only child of a divorced mother and doting grandparents. As an elementary school kid, Larry was chubby and a little cautious, but later when he grew into adolescence and lost his baby fat, became more adventurous and an excellent high school athlete.

The four of us did a lot of things together. We all felt comfortable with each other and our roles within the group. There was no competition for the alpha position and everyone was usually up for whatever the group wanted to do. Larry was sometimes hesitant to do things like go down to the riverbank because he was afraid his mother would find out and be disappointed in him. But we could eventually convince him his mother would not find out about it if he kept his mouth shut, because we were not going to tell anyone. He caught on quickly enough.

By 1954, our parents had stopped driving us to the movies and gave us twenty cents for bus fare, ten cents for the ticket to East Liverpool and ten cents for a return ticket to Newell. We each had twenty-five cents for admission and another fifteen cents to spend on refreshments. Candy was five cents a box and popcorn and pop were ten cents each. My wife, Liz, also a matinee movie fan, remembers that she chose her candy purchase by whether she wanted to eat it or throw it at other kids. Boston Baked Beans and Root Beer Barrels were the best to throw, she believed, because they were hard and not sticky. But Jujyfruits were good to eat because they tasted good and lasted a long time. Staying power was important in candy because, as a growing boy, I got really hungry watching all of those movies. By the end of the third hour I spent a nickel of my bus money for a Hershey Bar, confident that I could walk home across the bridge using my last nickel to pay the bridge toll.

But in that last hour a box of Good & Plenty, small licorice tubes covered with a hard pink or white sugar candy shell, began to call my name from the candy counter. I could not resist when the end of the box formed lips and whispered my name. A whisper that I could hear over the gunshots as another evildoer bit the dust at high noon. "Bobby," the voice insistently called. Mesmerized, I marched to the candy stand and plunked down my last nickel for that box of Good & Plenty. The other guys must have heard similar voices calling their names, because by the end of the afternoon we were all flat broke. We had spent our bus money and even the bridge toll money. We were forced to make the two mile walk home from East Liverpool, over the Newell Bridge that crossed the Ohio River. Unfortunately, without a nickel to pay the five-cent toll for walking the bridge our only option was to "run the bridge," which meant running past the bridge toll man without paying. We realized that if caught we could face jail time, a criminal record, and a life of crime that would inevitably follow.

Larry Hutton suggested that we call his mother who would drive over to East Liverpool and pick us up, but it hurt our pride too much to admit to an adult that we had been weak and given in to a box of candy. We would rather face the toll man than the look that Larry's mother would give us when we piled into her car, defeated by the temptation of the big-city theater.

The Newell Company, a wholly owned subsidiary of The Homer Laughlin China Company, owned the Newell Bridge and levied a toll of ten cents for cars and five cents for pedestrians. It might seem strange to have to pay a toll to walk across the bridge, but we never questioned it and just assumed that if cars paid, walkers should also pay. Apparently, most people paid the toll without questioning it because the Newell Bridge remains as one of the few privately owned toll bridges across the Ohio River.

The bridge spanned the river where it was very wide. It was at least half a mile long and fifty feet above the river. Crossing the bridge on foot was scary because the bridge shook when big trucks went across, and the bridge had a steel grating floor that you could look through and see the river below. Of course as elementary schoolboys, we didn't want to let the other guys know we were scared to walk the bridge.

Running the bridge was even scarier, but with no money we had no choice. The tollbooth was on the East Liverpool side of the river near the East Liverpool City Hospital. The street made a ninety-degree turn as it approached the bridge, and about fifty feet from the bridge there was an alley with a high hedge. About a block before the bridge street we ducked into the alley and sneaked along the hedge to the end of the alley. We hid behind the hedge waiting for the toll taker to go into the tollhouse on the side of the bridge for a cup of coffee or perhaps to eat some tollhouse cookies. We kept peeking around the hedges and breaking into uncontrolled nervous giggling. We hit the giggler on the arm and put our fingers to our lips in the universal sign to shut up, but that only invoked more giggling. We kept our vigil until at last the bridge man took a break and seemed to be securely in the tollhouse with no cars coming either way. Someone, I think it was Bob Shenton who was the oldest of the bunch, yelled, "Go!" and all four of us spread out and ran at top speed past the tollbooth. When we passed the tollbooth, Bob who was brave, yelled, "Ya Ya, we are running the bri-idge." The rest of us joined in but only after we were further onto the bridge and a safe distance from the tollbooth. The toll taker came out of the tollbooth on the run and yelled, "You kids are in trouble; I am going to call the police, and you will all go to jail."

We ran to the middle of the bridge and stopped briefly, out of breath. We threw pebbles we had picked up for just that purpose and our empty candy boxes way down into the water. Then we tried to spit. It was really exciting because a towboat passed below and we could see the men working and the waves the boat made. By the time we had crossed the bridge and had walked past the "Newell Unincorporated" sign, we were still high on sugar and adrenaline. We had faced down the twin challenges of walking the bridge and eluding the toll man.

I ran the bridge three or four times in my childhood and was never close to being caught by the toll man. In fact the only person I know of who was ever caught was Rick Brenneman, who had a girlfriend in East Liverpool and ran the bridge every night in his car. Eventually the toll man got so tired of seeing the same blue Nash Rambler run past his booth without paying that he called the Hancock County deputies with Rick's license plate number. The deputies paid a call on Rick and his parents, who were mortified, and he never ran the bridge again.

In retrospect, I wonder if the toll man really wanted to catch us. He must have seen four kids peeking around the hedge at the edge of the alley or heard us laughing. Why didn't the Newell Company hire younger, faster toll men to catch bridge runners? And, why didn't the toll man call the East Liverpool police who could easily apprehend us before we walked a half-mile to the other side of the bridge? Funny, none of those questions ever occurred to us back then.

———

I was shocked at how quickly television affected movies. By the mid-fifties, people who only five years before had gone to the movies on a weekly basis were staying home to watch television. Theaters in small towns began to limit their hours of operation and some even closed completely. Many of the theaters where I had watched movies, the Strand and Rex in Follansbee and the Alpine in Chester, closed before I got out of junior high school. The American Theater in East Liverpool did try to continue the kiddie matinees, but when I went to one in 1956, there were fewer than a dozen other kids rattling around in the huge theater. With so few kids cheering and throwing candy, there wasn't much energy or excitement. Although children's matinees were revived in the 1960s using full length cartoon features, they weren't the same.

Even though the golden age of movies had passed, four theaters continued to survive in East Liverpool by showing films in the evening to much smaller crowds. When I was in high school I occasionally took dates to movies like *A Summer Place* or *West Side Story*, but the three drive-in movies in the area were much more popular with teenagers for dates because there was more opportunity for innocent intimacy in the front seat of a car than in a darkened movie theater.

Later, Peter Bogdanovich's 1971 movie *The Last Picture Show*, my favorite movie of all time, captured this same time period in the fictional Texas town of Archer City. The film equated the closing of the movie theater with the loss of innocence. Little did we know how the fantasy world of movies had protected us from realities of war, crime, and poverty that soon were brought into our living rooms every night by television.

The speed with which TV became a staple in every home was astounding. The second era of television began in 1952, when the Federal Communications Commission lifted the rule that allowed only one station in most viewing areas. By 1953 WSTV-TV and WTRF-TV came on the air in Steubenville and Wheeling, giving people in Newell a choice of three different programs to watch in any time slot instead of just one.

One of the first victims of the multiple-channel era in TV was *The Voice of Firestone*. When the first chords of the Voice came on, there was an almost audible click all over America as people turned their channel selectors to another channel. The Firestone Company continued to sponsor *The Voice of Firestone* for eleven years despite low ratings. Finally, the network cancelled the show, even though the Firestone Company wanted to continue sponsoring it. The Voice's ratings were so abysmally low they hurt the programs that followed later in the evening.

Television shows became better because there was competition among stations for viewers. One of my favorite shows from this era was *The Wonderful World of Disney*, which premiered in 1954. I was eleven-years old when the series began, Jimbo was five and Janie was three. We expected to see one hour of wall-to-wall Disney cartoons, but were surprised when an early show of the series told the history of the Disney studios and demonstrated how animated cartoons were made. The show was fascinating. Later shows introduced full-length cartoons, showed how the movie *20,000 Leagues Under the Sea* was made, and introduced a series of movies about the frontiersman, Davy Crockett. Even my parents loved *The Wonderful World of Disney*.

Children's television changed quickly with the introduction of the *Mickey Mouse Club*. The club featured a cast of children who could sing, dance, and enjoy adventures. The show occasionally had animated cartoons, and later added a series of films about the adventures of Spin and Marty who were pre-adolescents. The show was kind of bland but a step up from Howdy Doody because it emphasized friendship and wholesome activities. I was just a little old for Mickey Mouse, I was really more of the Howdy Doody generation, but Jimbo and Janie were huge *Mickey Mouse Club* fans, complete with sets of the mouse ears.

The television programs we watched as a family were comedies like *I Love Lucy, The Ernie Kovacs Show, The Jack Benny Show,* and *The Life of Riley.* Adult westerns such as *Gunsmoke, Have Gun will Travel,* and *Wagon Train* became popular later in the decade. We also really liked dramatic programs like *Perry Mason, Alfred Hitchcock Theatre* and *Dragnet.* My family was hooked on television; it was turned on from the time we got up in the morning until we went to bed at night.

By far the most popular and enduring television show of the 1950s was the Sunday night *Ed Sullivan Show,* a variety program that featured everything from jugglers and people who spun plates to popular singers and comedians. In 1956 our family took our seats in the living room at 8:00 on Sunday night to watch Ed Sullivan introduce the controversial new singing sensation, Elvis Presley, to the mainstream public. Mom had threatened to not allow Jimbo, Janie, and me to watch because Elvis had the reputation of moving his hips suggestively, but she relented. My family along with 60 million other people (an astounding 82 percent audience share), watched Elvis from the waist up, because the censor's office did not want to expose the nation to Elvis shaking his hips. My friends and I did not see what was so suggestive about Elvis. We were thirteen and did not understand the nuances of sex. However, that show marked the end of sexual innocence in America. My parents like others in their generation wanted to hide sex and to pretend it did not exist. Their objection to Elvis and the absurd actions of the censors were a national public admission, for the first time, that sex existed and that it was bad for us for some reason. That of course made our teenage, hormone-racked bodies even more interested in the topic.

Television news in the early 1950s was not much different from news on the radio. TV news shows were mostly shots of an anchorman reading the news because it was so cumbersome to shoot film and get it on the air on a timely basis. The news shows were only fifteen minutes long, limiting the time that could be devoted to any one story. Nevertheless, early television network news programs were the beginning of our receiving consistent national and world news, and the network news programs got better with practice.

One of the highlights of television news during the 1950s was its coverage of the presidential conventions. My family did not have a television set for the 1952 convention, so 1956 was my first convention experience. I was thirteen-years old and my parents let me stay up to watch "history being made." The speeches were really boring but I loved to watch the delegates demonstrate for their candidates. Chet Huntley and David Brinkley who established their reputations at the 1952 conventions were the news anchor team at the convention for NBC, our favorite channel. The correspondents' interviews and the background information provided by the anchormen were extremely interesting and I felt privy to inside information. That convention was my first experience with the feeling I could learn more about something from watching television than if I were actually there. Television put me closer to the heart of the event.

The Democrats met first in 1956 in Chicago, where they nominated Adlai Stevenson again, on the first ballot. Stevenson threw the convention open for the selection of a vice-presidential candidate. The vice-presidential race was between the veteran Estes Kefauver and the youthful John F. Kennedy. It took Kefauver a rare second ballot vote to win the nomination. My parents let me stay up past 11:00 to hear the roll call voting, to me the most exciting part of the convention. We sat in our living room with our windows and front door open to catch the evening breeze, because the summer day had been sweltering. All up and down our street we could see the flickering glow of television sets through the front room windows and hear the muffled sounds of other televisions tuned into the same program we were watching. I felt very close to my parents that night because they included me in an adult event and I could listen to the adult conversation between them.

Later that summer in San Francisco, the Republicans nominated President Eisenhower on the first ballot. My father was a Republican and my mother a Democrat, so I was torn about whom I would support. I decided to support Ike, because how could I vote against the general who had won the war for us and was the president of the United States?

Most people in small towns knew only what they had learned through personal experience. Because the world of Newell was small and insular, we did not have much personal experience about national events. Most of them seemed to occur far away and to have very little impact on life in Newell. Consequently, most of the events of national importance in the 1950s went right past me and most of my friends. Television news was beginning to change that. Even though I never watched the Sunday afternoon documentaries because I had more interesting things to do, I frequently watched at least part of the evening news programs. Those programs were beginning to bring the world into living rooms in Newell in a way that made far away events part of our personal experiences.

Until I began watching television news programs, like most

people in Newell I knew little about civil rights. My first brush with civil rights had been when a sign appeared in the window of Mike's Tavern, a neighborhood bar in Newell's lower end. The hand-lettered sign, put up shortly after the racetrack opened, read, "We cater to white trade only." I had to ask my Dad what that meant. I was surprised when he carefully explained that Negroes were barred from Mike's. I was surprised; I believed Newell was a wonderful example of the melting pot of America because we had a lot of immigrants and first generation Italians and Poles living there. I believed we had all the major religions represented with Presbyterians, Methodists, Nazarenes, and Roman Catholics. Just as major league baseball believed it was America's game despite patently excluding African-Americans before 1947, I felt Newell was a wonderful example of America's melting pot despite not having any Jews, Hispanics, or Negroes as we called African-Americans in those days.

In fact, I had seen only one African-American in Newell before I was in junior high school. That person was also the most famous person I had ever seen in Newell. It was a gloomy, late spring Saturday when I was in either fifth or sixth grade. I was just wandering around looking for something interesting to do when I casually looked in the window of the Thornberry Brothers Grocery and saw the most famous person ever to visit Newell: Aunt Jemima. I could not believe my eyes, but there she was, just like her picture on the pancake mix packages. She was a large, African-American woman dressed in a white blouse with red polka dots and a floor length, full black skirt with a kerchief tied around her head.

Curious, I went inside to see what kind of major event was in progress. Aunt Jemima was standing behind a large griddle ready to make pancakes. I was shocked to see that there wasn't anyone else around. I just stood and stared at her, struck dumb in the presence of someone so famous. Obviously a professional,

Aunt Jemima asked me if I wanted a pancake. Of course I said yes; I was a kid who was always hungry and would eat anything. I was thrilled, because there I was standing right in Thornberry Brothers Grocery and the famous Aunt Jemima was making me a pancake with her very own mix.

I expected her to tell jokes like Amos and Andy did on the radio or to dispense stories which taught a lesson like Uncle Remus did in storybooks, because those were the only experiences I had had with African-Americans. But, she cooked in silence. The silence was oppressive, so to make conversation I asked, "How long have you been doing this?" "About six months," she replied. She served the pancake on a paper plate with syrup and gave me a plastic fork. "Thank you," I said as I gobbled down the pancake. She watched me eat in silence.

Later that afternoon I saw Aunt Jemima standing at the bus stop across the street from the grocery store. I said hello, but she didn't seem to remember me even though we had met only a couple hours before; she seemed kind of nervous. I was really surprised that someone as famous as Aunt Jemima had to take the bus, instead of having someone drive her in a car. And I wondered why she was going to East Liverpool.

The only other experience I had with African-Americans was in playing sports. The year following the 1954 Brown v. Board of Education Supreme Court decision that mandated integration of public schools, Hancock County fully integrated its schools. This decision did not directly affect Newell because we did not have any African-Americans living in our town. However, six African-American students, who lived in Chester and had previously been bused to East Liverpool since Ohio schools were integrated, were allowed to attend school in Chester. In Weirton, in the southern end of Hancock County where my cousins went to school, integration was a significant event. About five percent of the population of

Weirton was African-American, and the town's elementary and secondary schools had both been segregated. Integration in Weirton went smoothly, according to my cousins, for two reasons. A number of excellent African-American athletes began playing for Weir High School and led them to state championships. The Weirton Steel Company, then the biggest employer in West Virginia, employed a significant number of African-Americans and wanted to keep them happy. What the coaches and the mill wanted, everyone in Weirton wanted.

The first time I competed against African-American kids was in seventh grade (1955 - 56) when the Cove Junior High School basketball team from Weirton came to Newell to play our seventh and eighth grade teams. The Cove coach was African-American as was about one-third of the team. They were very tall and athletic and scored almost at will, beating us easily; but none of the players showed off or acted in anything other than a sportsmanlike way. I found that to be true with all the African-Americans I played against in junior high, high school, and college sports.

I did not have many other sources of information about African-Americans. Mrs. George, my social studies teacher, told us that the African-Americans she went to school with in East Liverpool were neat, clean, and on their best behavior. My parents told me that African-Americans were people just like us. When I asked people in Newell who were openly against African-Americans why they felt that way, they mumbled something like, "they smell bad, are lazy, and clannish." That could have described me, most of my friends, and a lot of the other people who lived in Newell.

Television provided more information than I could have found in Newell. Although the few African-Americans on early television played stereotyped roles, as the decade progressed, African-Americans were shown with increasing frequency. *The Nat King Cole Show* was the first show hosted by an African-American. Rock and roll was a huge boon to African-Americans; singers like Johnny Mathis and groups like the Platters, the Coasters, the Drifters, and Little Anthony and the Imperials were being increasingly featured on variety shows and *American Bandstand.*

Televised sports featured African-Americans. I watched Jackie Robinson lead the Brooklyn Dodgers to National League pennants and a World Series win over the New York Yankees; Marion Motley and Bill Willis star on the World Champion Cleveland Browns; and Wilt Chamberlain and Hal Greer spark Philadelphia to a National Basketball Association Championship, in the rare year that they beat the Boston Celtics with Bill Russell and Sam Jones. In the 1950s those players and many other African-Americans became stars in integrated sports. More importantly, I saw hundreds of other African-Americans playing on professional and college teams as teammates with white athletes. I was a huge sports fan so that left a powerful message with me. I respected the talent and effort the African-American athletes displayed. I was even more impressed with the African-American and white players working smoothly together as teammates.

As the decade progressed the network news programs got better at using film for breaking stories. The 1956 Birmingham bus boycott and the denial of admission to an African-American student, Autherine Lucy, to the University of Alabama began to catch my attention, but I really could not understand the issues and they were not well explained in the limited time allotted to the stories. However, in 1957 when Governor Orval Faubus of Arkansas would not allow nine African-American students to enter Little Rock Central High School, I became intrigued with the story because those kids were my age, and I did not need any explanation for what I saw. The television news showed nine scared African-American kids bravely facing down an ugly, angry white mob. Even through a twenty-one-inch blurry black and white television screen, I could feel the hatred of the crowd, many of whom were women. The crowd spit, swore, and surged forward looking as if it could break into mob violence at any minute despite the presence of the National Guard. I had never before seen such raw anger and hatred. I could not believe that Americans could treat other Americans that way just because of skin color.

The fifteen-minute news programs were not good at sorting out the complex issues of race. I could not understand why the African-American students wanted to integrate where they were not wanted. Likewise, I could not understand why white people were so enraged by nine nice, clean-cut African-Americans wanting to go their school.

Neither television nor anything else solved the issue of school integration in the 1950s because as late as 1964 only 2.3 percent of African-American children in the south went to integrated schools. Television did not answer my questions, but instead suggested to me that African-Americans were people of talent and could work well together with white people. Also I began to realize how deep racial hatred ran in the United States and how ugly it was. Later, in the 1960s, television would become an even more powerful force in shaping public opinion about race in America.

During the decade of the 1950s the United States moved from being a radio and movie country to a television country. In 1950 there were only 3.9 million television homes in the United States (about 9 percent of the American homes). By 1960 television had saturated the country. That year the United States had 45.8 million television sets in 87.5 percent of the homes. In Newell we were no longer an isolated outpost. We were wired to the world. We were no longer influenced just by what our neighbors thought; instead the opinions and experiences of people in the rest of the country shaped our ideas. We were no longer ignorant hicks; we were tuned into the trends that were sweeping the nation. We had seen the dark side of humankind. Crime, hate, violence, sex, and evil were shown in our living rooms each night, not only on the news but also on regular evening programs. We learned much from television, but it came at the loss of innocence, just one more breakdown in the life of small town America.

BOTTOM ROW, L-R - Bob Barnett, Glen Phillips, Eugene Hart, Joe Fuller, Larry Hutton, Dewey McPherson, Ronald Noland, Logan Six, Tom Woods.
ROW 2, L-R - Jake Geer, Kip Smith, Jim Reed, Rick Webb, Tom Lemasters, Gary Daugherty, Bill Monroe, Dave Phillips, Dave Bell, Manager, Tom Robison.
ROW 3, L-R - Paul Arnott, Harry Emmerling, Sonny Rice, Rick Anderson, Bill Bell, Joe Hall, James Seevers, Ed Wiersbicki, Mickey Staley.
ROW 4, L-R - Gary Rayle, Richard Goppert, Terry Robinson, Sam Simmons, Tom Franczek.

Football

SEASON'S RECORD

NEWELL		OPPONENT
13	St. Anthony	27
6	New Cumberland	26
6	Hopedale	38
12	Wayne	47
13	South Side	19
13	Chester	25
0	Irondale	44
6	Salineville	18
20	Fairfield-Waterford	48

COACH HOROSZKO

The yearbook record of a dismal season. (Photo from the 1961 Newell High School Yearbook courtesy of Ruth and Joe Fuller)

Chapter 9

Friday Night Rites

Follansbee, where my life began, was genuine football territory. Playing football for the Follansbee Blue Wave served as a test of manhood and courage for every member of the team, but for the sons of Italian and Polish steel mill workers, a spot on the football team also signaled acceptance into the mainstream of American life. Every Friday night, it seemed as if the whole town packed the Follansbee High School stadium or followed their heroes to fields up and down the Ohio Valley. In this steel town, the drama of high school football was entertainment of the highest order in the pre-television era of the late 1940s. I didn't get to play for our beloved Blue Wave, because my parents moved to Newell when I was in second grade. Yet my parents and I continued to make the Friday pilgrimage down the Ohio River to wherever the Blue Wave was playing. As we drove along the river and darkness fell, we could tell which high schools were playing at home because the stadium lights shone above the two-story buildings. In the early 1950s, before the big push for school consolidation, every town up and down the river had its own high school. Most spectacular of all was the riverfront stadium at Toronto, Ohio, where lights cast shimmering streaks across the inky, placid river and illuminated

As a sophomore football player I did not strike fear in our opponents' hearts because I was tiny at 5'3" tall and 110 pounds. (Photo courtesy of *Goldenseal Magazine*)

the autumn leaves on the hillside rising above the other side of the stadium.

After each Follansbee home game, seven of my father's brothers and sisters, along with their husbands, wives, boyfriends, girlfriends, and children would gather at Grandma and Grandpa Barnett's. The noise and confusion were overpowering. Football talk mingled with a thick pall of smoke from unfiltered Luckies, Camels, Pall Malls, and Chesterfields. Sandwiches with Spam cut as thick as your finger were served along with strong, hot coffee. Uncle Dick always gave me a couple drinks of his coffee, which was black with four spoonfuls of sugar.

My chance at high school football glory came when I reached ninth grade and tried out for the Newell High School Big Green team. The school was so small, with fewer than eighty boys, that everyone who tried out, from ninth through twelfth grade, made the squad of twenty to thirty players. At five-feet even and ninety-six pounds, I was by far the smallest player on the team. All the equipment I was issued was too large and a chore just to carry on my body, except for the helmet, which was too small. I struggled manfully with this helmet every time I had to put it on. Sometimes it took me four or five minutes. Once on, it squeezed my head, smelled bad, and had an old-fashioned clear plastic facemask that obstructed my vision. Taking it off over my ears was equally time-consuming and painful, and sometimes made my ears bleed. This created a dilemma during the games. Should I sit on the bench with my helmet on in pain or risk being sent into the game and not being able to get it on by the time I reached the field? I need not have worried, because I played only about thirty seconds in the very last game of the season.

The next season I got a helmet that was only slightly too large with a nice double bar in the front. Direct hits caused the front of the helmet to cut the top of my nose. I spent the first two months of

I am making a diving catch after becoming an offensive machine in the 1959 game against New Waterford-Fairfield High School. Notice the large crowd attending the game.

my sophomore year with a scab on my nose, but the blood on my face gave me a tough "hard-nosed" look. Later, seniority allowed me to get helmets that fit.

⟶

The opening game of the season meant that we survived the hated two-a-day, preseason practices, but also that we were to be tested in public. The pre-game locker-room smelled of adolescent perspiration and Aqua Velva. The low murmur of the players was drowned out by the cleats scraping on the cement floor and the sound of water running from the showers, but particularly by the constant flushing of the urinals as players relieved their nervousness, some three or four times. Usually the urge came only when your uniform was completely laced up.

The pre-game pep talks were usually something along the lines of "you can win if you try and if you believe." However, the pre-game prayer was more inspirational. The coach intoned, "Let's repeat the Lord's Prayer." It started smoothly enough, but by the fourth line, "Thy Kingdom come," it began to take on the deep, staccato beat of the offensive signals. "Give us this day" was almost a guttural shout from deep in our throats, and the "Amen" was roared just before we screamed, "Let's get 'em" and broke for the door. Unfortunately, the door in our gym opened inward, somewhat slowing our progress and dampening our enthusiasm.

By my sophomore year in the fall of 1958, I had grown to five-feet, five-inches and weighed 110 pounds. We opened that season at Madonna, the Catholic high school in Weirton. We were somewhat disconcerted to start with, realizing that at a Catholic school they must pray more than we did. And screaming, "Beat Madonna" sounded somehow sacrilegious. If the game were close, would God take their side?

We needn't have worried because they ran the opening kickoff back for a touchdown and proceeded to score at will. We had to endure more than a sound beating, though. The Weirton stadium was built on a hill next to the Weirton Steel Company's open-hearth furnaces. By the third quarter, the score was in the fifties, and, with the open hearth spewing smoke, ash, and sparks into the hot humid September night, the game seemed endless. We began to feel as if we were perhaps dead and paying for our sins. Mercifully, the game ended with Newell on the short end of a 60 - 0 score. We were young men who had looked into the face of hell.

That defeat was our worst but not our last, for we were a small high school made up of sons of potters. Of course we couldn't beat steel town teams. Plus, our coach wasn't much of a football strategist. He was a wonderful man, a large, burly former lineman of Eastern European descent with a name of confusing Zs and Ks. His philosophy of life was to work hard, hunker down, and drive right through them.

Though his play calling left something to be desired, he insisted on sending plays into the game. In the early games, we ran the up the middle and off tackle, plays he called with a sincere and honest effort, but as the losses mounted, we began to snicker, then laugh out loud as the messenger brought in one failure after another. Finally we took control of our own fate and began calling our own plays. The coach didn't seem to notice that we ran different plays from those he sent in until the next to last game in my senior year. He confronted the quarterback in the locker room at halftime and asked why he had not run the "T-2-Ride" play that he sent in to the game. The room grew ominously silent. Mickey Staley, the quarterback, ever a quick thinker, looked levelly at the coach and said, "Reed forgot the play while he was running onto the field." The coach could relate to that and as a team we let out a sigh of relief.

Playing for a losing team was never a complete bummer. By the time my junior season rolled around, I had grown to five-feet, eight-inches and 125 pounds and was starting at end on offense and sometimes on defense. My younger brother, Jimbo, and his friends worshiped the ground I was knocked down on, and the high school girls, who never really seemed to understand the game, were just impressed that I played.

My aunts and uncles sometimes made the trip to Newell to see me play against other small town teams, such as Darlington (Pennsylvania), Irondale (Ohio), Salineville (Ohio), Cameron (West Virginia), New Cumberland (West Virginia), and of course our arch rival Chester. These games would end in a few years for almost all of them, including Newell, consolidated into large high schools during the 1960s and 1970s. After the first home game my family sat around our dining room table eating Spam and drinking coffee. Everyone made a fuss over me when I came in. I acted embarrassed, but I really swelled with pride, as I know they did also. "You'll get them next week," they encouraged as I got ready to leave for a post-game date. Just as I was leaving, Uncle Dick walked me to the door, made some small talk, and handed me a dollar, saying, "Have a good time." In 1959, you could. With that dollar, I bought my date and me hamburgers and milkshakes, which we enjoyed in the car at Hoge's Drive-In Restaurant.

The high point of high school football for me came in the last game of the 1959 season against New Waterford-Fairfield, Ohio. Near the end of the first half we were losing as usual, and in desperation the coach called a pass. I went downfield about seven yards from my left end position and cut sharply in front of the defensive halfback (that's what they were called then). As I made my cut, everything seemed to drift into slow motion. I could see the laces on the ball as it slowly spiraled towards me and into my hands. As I cut around the defender, I felt as if I were being swung on a string in the grip of some powerful centrifugal force. Once around the corner, I was in the clear. The wind whistled past the ear holes in my helmet and blurred my vision. I could see the goal post but it seemed to be a mile down the field. I was isolated and not conscious of anything except the goal line getting slowly closer. After what seemed like five minutes, I made it to the goal line with a sixty-five yard pass-run for a touchdown. As I turned in the end zone, I was startled to see other players still on the field. The rest of the game was equally exciting. I became an offensive weapon by catching five or six more passes, one of them a diving catch, but of course we lost again.

⟶

The game against our arch rival, the Chester High School Panthers, was a memorable moment during my senior year. Because Newell and Chester were only one mile apart, we were blood rivals in sports and almost everything else for that matter. We felt we were as good as, if not better than, Chester in every aspect of life. But if truth be told (and it hurt) Chester had twice as many people as Newell. They were incorporated; we weren't. They had sidewalks and nice streets; we had potholes and dirt paths. Undaunted by reason we believed our athletic teams were better and our girls prettier.

The last time anybody could remember beating Chester in football was 1954. No one could recall any other specific victory, but there were rumors of one sometime in the 1930s when the Newell coach had slipped down to the pottery at halftime for reinforcements. In some ways being an extreme underdog was not so bad. There was nothing to lose, and the occasional victory conferred instant status as legend. "He played on the team that beat Chester," old-timers would say when one of the Kiger brothers or Larry Foltz or Sonny Gregory walked past. All of them had been Newell players on that legendary 1954 Newell team.

We didn't do well against Chester in 1957 or 1958, my freshman and sophomore years, although I did catch two passes in the 1958 game. My accomplishment drove the Chester coach into such a rage that he pulled the whole defense from my side of the field to chew them out. They came back into the game with an intense look of determination on their faces. They proceeded to punish me as only experienced players could pound a 110-pound sophomore. I never held it against them. The glow of those passes and having my name in the newspaper the next day made my season.

The next year Chester had one of their best teams ever, losing only one game to a much larger school and even beating the tough Follansbee Blue Wave. Our only hope was to attack, even off the field. The night before the game two pickup trucks and a couple of cars loaded with our whole team and bushel baskets of overripe tomatoes invaded Chester territory.

The rest of the night was a blur. I recall driving through Chester at breakneck speed trying to hold onto the truck while hurling tomatoes at everything that moved. We met no opposition. The Chester players cowered in their homes, resting for the game. Later that night some of the Chester boys invaded Newell, but without the stores of tomatoes we had amassed, they failed to make a mark. It was a titanic battle—a smashing victory for us—fought in the very streets, sidewalks, and alleyways of the towns. In the game the next day, we went down to defeat by the humiliating score of 38 - 0. It didn't matter as we had made our point and the event will live in the lore of the Newell-Chester rivalry forever. Just mention The Great Tomato Fight to anyone of a certain age and a wistful smile will cross his lips as he recalls his role in the epic battle that fateful night.

The Chester-Newell game of 1960 was the last chance for us seniors to tear a shred of immortality from the sweatshirt of athletic glory. We hadn't won a game, but Chester was also having a rare down season. If we could somehow catch them by surprise perhaps we could pull off a monumental upset.

Every year Coach Horoszko would add something new to either the offense or defense during "Chester week." The 1960 season saw us install an eight-man defensive line and add a lonesome end offensive series, desperate measures by desperate men.

Actually, the new strategy almost worked. Near the end of the third quarter, we were ahead 13 - 7 and had moved to our thirty-five-yard line on a drive. Then the inevitable happened. They held us on downs, scored to tie the game, and came back in the fourth quarter to score two more touchdowns and win 28 - 13.

The sun came up the next morning, but the rivalry we expected to continue forever ended in 1963. That year Newell, Chester, and New Cumberland consolidated into Oak Glen High School. The rivalry ended sooner for me. That spring I fell in love with a girl from Chester. She is now my wife, and still prettier than any Newell girl.

My senior football picture when I was a much bigger at 5'8" tall and 125 pounds. (Photo courtesy of *Goldenseal Magazine*)

Chapter 10

The Worst Team Ever

My basketball career began in January of the fourth grade, the year after the championship season, when Coach Robison organized an elementary school intramural basketball league for fifth and sixth graders. Tom Woods, one of my classmates, and I wanted to play too. The second Saturday after the league was in operation, we showed up with everybody else. We walked into the locker room to taunts of, "What are you fourth graders doing here?" Once in the locker room, Tom and I huddled together to screw up enough courage to talk to the coach. After a couple minutes we knocked on the coaches' door. Two high school players who were acting as coaches answered the door and gruffly asked, "What do you want?" They had faint smiles on their faces, though, as two timid fourth graders asked to speak to Coach Robison. We were ushered into the inner office, a small, smoke-filled cubicle hardly big enough for the one desk that all of the Newell coaches shared. The walls were covered with aging brown newspaper clippings and team pictures thumb-tacked directly onto the wallboard. Haltingly we made our case, but confessed that we were only fourth graders. We showed Coach Robison our gym shorts and the shoes our mothers had carefully packed for us the night before. "Sure," said the man with a soft spot in his heart for kids who loved basketball. "We can put you on teams today."

I was assigned to the American Legion team and Tom was put on the Fire Department team. My team jersey was yellow with navy blue lettering. The smallest size they had left was a men's size thirty-four, given to me even though I wore a boy's size twelve. The shirt hung down to my knees. "Perfect fit," the high school boy who coached the American Legion team said. "It will give you lots of room to move around." The other high school boys laughed, but I didn't care; I was on my first team with my first uniform.

I rolled the shirt up and tucked it in my shorts so it would hang just a little below my shorts. I ran up the locker room steps to the gym floor, as I would do hundreds of times in years to come. The last four steps from the seating level to the gym floor took me from the common ground where mortals walked to the floor where the champs had played only the season before. I paused at the door; the highly polished floor looked beautiful reflecting the morning light that shone through the heavy glass block windows. I ran onto the floor but quickly looked back to see if I was leaving footprints. I was on hallowed ground. The rest of the morning was a blur.

When the game was over, I ran all the way home to show Mom and Dad my new shirt. They smiled when I put it on. Dad said it was almost his size, and Mom said she could wear it to do spring-cleaning. But I could tell beneath the teasing they were pleased and proud I had taken the initiative and successfully joined the world of team sports.

Robbie, as Coach John Robison was affectionately known, was a unique man. At about 6'6" he was easily the tallest man in town and taller by far than any of his players. Because of his height and build he resembled Abe Lincoln without the beard and mole.

He told us he had not been a very good basketball player in high school because he played in the late 1930s when coaches did not know how to use big men effectively. But we suspected he was also slow and not well coordinated.

His height made him stand out in any crowd and made it difficult for him to buy suits. Once he wore a stunning new gabardine plaid suit to a game for the first time. When he emerged from the locker room and walked across the floor, the crowd rose to its feet and gave him a standing ovation. That is the only time I had ever seen a suit get a standing O. Coach Robison ignored the cheers as coaches always did then.

Coach Robison, with a math degree from Fairmont State College and a Master's degree from Columbia University, was a very bright man with a keen, analytical mind. I don't know what possessed him to come to Newell as a high school math teacher and coach except that he loved kids and basketball. He understood the sport on many levels, and could see perfect games played out in his head. No doubt the championship team was the height of his career, when those perfect games were also played out on the floor. Only a few years later the teams I played on were clearly a challenge to his patience and skill as a coach. He never yelled at us or derided us, but instead sat stoically on the bench, arms folded, and long legs wrapped around each other. He looked like Plastic Man from the comic books. He added to the effect by rubbing the loose skin on his face up and down. But a good play on the floor would cause him to unwind a couple of turns, slap his knee, break into an infectious grin, and say to the subs on the bench, "Did you see that? Now that's how you're supposed to play."

Robbie loved kids. He spent numerous hours with us at practice, had us to his house to listen to audiotapes of the games, and took us to college basketball games despite the fact we lost frequently.

His pet peeve was players who went to dances, dated girls, and fell in love. He warned us that when players were in love they would "moon around and not be able to concentrate on basketball." More than once, he told us the cautionary tale of a player on the championship team who fell in love until the rest of the team sat him down and told him to cut it out until after the season. He listened to them and broke up with his girl until after the championship game. We listened, but we were weak. We went to dances and chased girls with the same zeal we chased rebounds. Larry Hutton, the team's ladies' man, practiced dance steps outside the coaches' room just to drive them crazy.

Tom Woods, Mick Staley, Ron Noland, Larry Hutton, and I worked our way up through Newell's basketball system from church league to junior high to freshman team to the reserve team and eventually the varsity. Tom Bell joined us in our junior season when he transferred from Wheeling. We all had a little bit of talent for the game; even me. I occasionally started games, and once or twice played a starring role, but I also had a number of liabilities. In ninth grade I was five-feet tall and grew to only five-feet, eight-inches by my senior year. In addition, I was skinny, slow, and could not jump very high. The only thing I had going for myself was that I practiced all the time, even going down to my basement at night after the regular practice at school to dribble between chairs and do ball-handling drills.

During my sophomore year in 1958 - 59, Tom, Mick, Ron, Larry, and I made the varsity, because the juniors and seniors were not very good. What a thrill it was to run onto the floor with the varsity in a beautiful fleecy white warm-up suit and do the same pre-game drills the championship team had done only seven years before. But any comparison between the state champions and us ended there. Wellsville crushed us in the opening game of the season by

I am scrambling for a loose ball in a 1961 game. Notice my tongue sticking out even before Michael Jordan started that trend—but I did not hustle enough to dive to the floor for the ball. (Photo from the 1961 Newell High School Yearbook courtesy of Ruth and Joe Fuller)

the humiliating score of 69 - 18. I got to play almost half the game as Coach Robison substituted freely, but we were clearly pathetic and embarrassed in front of the whole town.

Even Coach Robison was shocked at how inept we were. In desperation he combined the reserve and varsity teams for practice, and used most of us sophomores as starters on the reserve team so that we could get game experience and feel what it was like to win. Against some teams I played the entire reserve game and half the varsity game. We got a lot of playing experience and won most of the reserve games.

Coach Robison decided he needed to return to teaching us very basic basketball skills. We drilled over and over on dribbling, passing, and basic defense. Over Christmas vacation we practiced twice a day for two hours at each practice. We worked on the classic three man fast break, a technique I can still do in my sleep. We made thousands of trips up and down the floor at breakneck speed. We were so exhausted from practice the team was actually happy to see Christmas vacation end and school start again.

By our tenth straight loss, a 66 - 38 crush by Beaver Local (Ohio) High School, Coach Robison gave up on winning and just hoped we would do something to indicate we were learning good basketball. But good plays were few and far between. He substituted often to try to find the best combination of players, but nothing worked. I even got enough playing time to earn a varsity letter, but players on the other teams would often snicker when I ran out on the court because I was so small at five-feet, three-inches and 110 pounds.

When the losses hit fourteen in a row, with a particularly embarrassing 101 to 59 loss to Bethany (West Virginia) High School, a school so small they did not have enough boys for a football team, Newell began a contest to select a new school nickname. Somehow the name Big Green did not fit us; maybe a new name would change our luck. After surveying the town and allowing the students to debate and vote, we assumed the name Vikings. Despite the new name, however, we were the same old team. We ended the regular season with our nineteenth straight loss, an 81 - 59 debacle at the hands of Jefferson Union (Ohio) High School. That season's record was the worst in Newell High School history. It must have been a long fall for Coach Robison to go from state champion to a winless season in seven years, but he handled it with grace and class.

We opened sectional tournament play against West Liberty High School, and miraculously beat them 76 - 66 to advance to the sectional championship game. Sadly, the glory was short-lived as New Cumberland crushed us once again 83 - 43 to end that nightmare season.

The 1959 - 60 season, my junior year, was better. We won our fifth game of the season by beating Beaver Local 61 - 53. We went on to defeat our arch rival Chester twice that season, something even the championship team did not accomplish. Our final record was seven wins and fourteen losses.

During that season I had a fleeting vision of how basketball was played at a higher level. I was again playing on the second team behind Tom Woods, Larry Hutton, Mickey Staley, Bob Stine, Ron Noland, and Tom Bell, but I was starting all the reserve games most often as a point guard. Unfortunately, I had sprained my ankle in a preseason practice and missed the first six games of the season. Watching from the bench with my leg in a cast, I mentally rehearsed what I would do when I was able to play. Finally, when the cast came off, I was able to join the team. I still had a noticeable limp, but was eager to play.

During the third game after coming back from the injury I had the most phenomenal game of my career. I was playing point guard in a reserve game, at home, against Jefferson Union. The second time down the court I took a jump shot from the top of the key (free-throw circle for younger fans) that swished the net and felt clean and smooth as it came off my hand. Twice more down the floor produced two more baskets. I quit looking to pass and only looked for the basket; everything I threw up went in and everything I tried worked. It was as if I was playing at normal speed, but the rest of the game was in slow motion. The other team began to foul to stop me, but the shots continued to drop. One shot was two feet too high, but hit the backboard and went in. Another time I was knocked down while shooting, but the ball somehow went in the basket. I even made twelve of fourteen foul shots even though I was usually lucky to make 50 percent in practice. I scored thirty-two points in a twenty-four-minute game, which we won easily. That was a golden game—a game in which I could do no wrong.

Two! I am shooting a 15 foot jump shot against Beaver Local in a 1960 game.

The *East Liverpool Review* wrote, "Bob Barnett, who is just getting over his foot injury, waxed red hot."

But nobody made too much of it, because that was a time when everyone was cool and did not show emotion. They also did not want me to get conceited or have "a big head."

Unfortunately, I never came close to duplicating that performance. I had some good games, but never scored twenty points again. I sank back to being a short, slow point guard who could not jump and was an average shooter.

Near the end of the season I began to question why I was even playing basketball. I liked being on the team, I liked the games, and Mom and Dad were proud that I was on the team. But I did not like being shut up in the gym for two hours every day after school and the practices were long and hard. I realized I did not have much talent or much feel for the game. But what was the alternative? I didn't like riding around in cars, or hanging out at the Shamrock Restaurant, or watching *American Bandstand* on television. If I quit the team I would probably end up just playing basketball on an outdoor court after school; so why not stay with the team, inside where it was warm and dry? I realized I would never be good enough to earn a college scholarship and probably would never be a starter, but playing on the team was better than the other choices, so I resolved to make the best of it. Deep in my heart, I knew that I loved football, liked baseball, but was only friends with basketball.

The 1960 - 61 season, my senior year, was really satisfying. Seniors and starters did not play in the reserve games, but lounged in the back row of the stands until midway in the third quarter of the reserve game when we sauntered casually to the locker room amid cheers of encouragement. After the reserve game we raced out onto the court in our white fleece warm-ups to do the time honored two-line lay-up drill, and then the four-man weave lay-up drill just as the championship team had done nine years before. I was the sixth man, and got to play in every game. Occasionally I started if someone was sick or injured. I was even the captain for one game against Salineville (Ohio) High School.

Best of all, we were finally winners. Midway through the season we had a fancy eight win, two loss record and were scheduled to play undefeated Stanton Local (Ohio) High School in the featured game of the week. The game was broadcast over WOHI radio station and Bob Duffy, the *East Liverpool Review*'s sports editor, covered the game. When I ran out on the floor that night I was thrilled to see the main floor seats filled and the band balcony, opened by the principal, Mr. Slack, also nearly full. That was the biggest crowd I had ever seen at Newell, except for the Wellsville and Chester games during the championship season.

Unfortunately, Stanton Local had an excellent team led by an

The 1960 - 61 Newell Vikings basketball team finished with a respectable 13 - 8 record. (Left to right) front row: Coach Robison, Tom Woods, David Reed, Mickey Staley, Ron Noland, and Dave Shilling; back row: manager Tom Robison, Dave Bell, the author, Larry Hutton, Kip Smith, and Jim Johnson. (Photo from the 1961 Newell High School Yearbook courtesy of Joe and Ruth Fuller)

agile 6'7" center. He towered over Tom Woods and Mickey Staley, our tallest players, who were about 6'1" each. I barely came to his chest. On top of that, he could play. Stanton Local easily beat us, 59 - 45.

We slid to five wins and five losses for the rest of the season to finish the year with a respectable thirteen win, eight loss record. Three of the losses were to New Cumberland, which beat us twice during the regular season and again in the first game of the sectional tournament. They went all the way to the area tournament finals, only one game from the state tournament. Our consolation was that we played them close; we lost by only five points each game during the regular season. We had a winning record and beat our arch rival Chester twice during the season, so all in all it was a success.

I enjoyed the season, but there was little sadness when it ended in early March. We had so much to look forward to, like baseball, the prom, commencement, summer vacation, and college in the fall, and I had just started dating a very attractive and interesting girl from Chester who would later become my wife.

⁓

Some people contend being a high school athlete is the best time in life. Not true. Things like getting married, earning college degrees, having children, and writing books are just as good. But being a high school player does validate you as a person of skill and worth at a fragile time in your life, when you move from adolescence toward adulthood and need the confidence to make big steps and big decisions. Plus, how can you top having a beautiful cheerleader jump up and down, kick her legs, pump her arms and lead the crowd in saluting you with the cheer,

> *Knit one,*
> *Purl two!*
> *Bob Barnett—*
> *Woo woo!*

Worker on the glaze belt at The Homer Laughlin China Company, c. 1950s. (Photo courtesy of The Homer Laughlin China Company)

Chapter 11
Work

When I was in junior high school, my parents gave me a weekly allowance of one dollar. This wasn't bad for junior high school; my biggest expenses were the thirty-five cents admission to Newell High School football and basketball games and the twenty cents for popcorn and a coke at the games. Then there was the nickel a day for candy, the nickel a week for Sunday school collection, and the occasional seven cents for a six-ounce bottle of soda pop. Tickets for the major school dances, such as the Christmas dance, were $1.50, so I had to save up for those extraordinary events. In high school my parents raised my allowance to two dollars a week. When I worked on summer jobs they stopped my allowance, and except for five dollars a week, they made me save the rest of my pay for college.

High school was expensive because of dating. In those years, men and boys paid for everything on a date. I went to the Chester Hi-Teen dance every week. Hi-Teen cost twenty-five cents, and if I took a girl home afterward, the stop at Hoge's Restaurant cost a dollar for two hamburgers and two milkshakes. Fortunately I did not have to pay for football or basketball games, since I was playing in them. But if I wanted to do anything else, I had to work the usual teenage jobs like cutting grass and shoveling snow. In fact, most summers I had a couple of regular grass cutting customers who paid me between fifty cents and $1.25 depending on the size of their yard.

I liked snow when I was a child because I enjoyed sledding, but when I hit junior high I loved snow. Then I could make big bucks shoveling people's sidewalks and driveways. If the snow was deep enough I might get four or five shoveling jobs and make as much as five dollars, more than double my weekly allowance. I was rich.

Not many jobs were available for teenagers during the school year. Fast food was yet to be invented, so places like McDonald's or Subway didn't exist. Bob Stine worked part-time at Raymond's Grocery Store and John Jennings and Mary Nease worked at Carnahan's Drug Store; other than that, there were no part-time jobs during the school year. The situation for girls was both better and worse. Girls could easily get work babysitting, but it didn't pay much money.

In the summers during the late '40s and early '50s, high school and college boys could always get summer jobs at either Weirton Steel or Homer Laughlin. Both paid good money, but by the middle '50s the boom was over. The demise of those summer jobs signaled the beginning of the decline of heavy industry in America.

Some Newell boys, like Joe Graham and Tom Woods, worked at the racetrack as hot walkers in the summer, walking the horses to cool them down after their morning training. Hot walking did not appeal to me. I did not relish the thought of getting up at 6:00 in the morning, and I was afraid the horses would kick or bite me.

Turning sixteen in my sophomore year meant I could get my driver's license and a full-time summer job. My friends Bill Moffitt and Larry Hutton and I talked over the situation. We figured that if we worked a forty-hour week at minimum wage (at that time $1.10), we would make $44.00 a week. That was an unheard of amount for a rising high school junior.

The problem was where to get a job. We had no idea what we wanted to do, or how to go about finding work. Mom stepped in and made things work for me, as she so often did. She was the executive secretary for James F. Edwards, who owned the Waterford Park racetrack. Because the horses raced for only about six or eight weeks in the summer and six or eight weeks in the fall or spring, Mom's job was just part-time. Outside of the two racing seasons, she worked only a couple other weeks during the year. The rest of the time she drew unemployment. The unemployment office occasionally called with job leads, but Mom never followed up because she liked working at the racetrack. She was happy to work four or five months a year and then ride in her best friend's Cadillac to sign up for her monthly unemployment check. She voted Democratic, and was actually able to get a job as a poll worker through the Democratic Party. My Republican dad railed at the welfare system, but never objected to Mom's cashing her unemployment checks.

In May, Berlo Caterers, which ran the restaurants and concession stands at Waterford Park, conducted interviews for food workers for the summer racing season. Mom drove me to the racetrack so I could interview. I was excited because the racetrack was located in a beautiful park-like setting and had the glamour of gambling attached. I thought the racetrack was where things were happening, but I later realized that I could have been working at any cafeteria and the job would have been about the same.

Hundreds of people were being interviewed. I felt very adult, but had no idea this was the first step to ending my carefree childhood. I completed the application and the interview went fine.

Two weeks later I was called and told to report as a cafeteria busboy on June 15, 1959, a date that will also live in infamy.

When I reported to work on the appointed day, Mrs. Zagula, the boss and my friend Theresa's mom, fleshed out the details of the job. There were three busboys, Chuck Laughlin and Jon Lombardo, both from Hookstown, Pennsylvania, and myself. Chuck had just graduated from Chester High School and Jon was a rising senior at South Side (Pennsylvania) High School, so I was the kid of the bunch. We had to work six days a week from 9:00 to 6:00. We worked longer than everyone else because we had to mop the floor after the cafeteria closed. The pay was ninety cents an hour, less than minimum wage, but we earned $48.60 a week plus tips, which wasn't bad. My mom made only $60 for a 48-hour workweek; women's salaries were low even when they held important jobs.

Everything seemed fine until the work began. For the 9:00 to 11:00 period we had to sweep the floor, take the chairs down from the tables, fill the napkin holders and salt and pepper shakers, make a commissary run to pick up supplies, and clean the cafeteria trays. There must have been a thousand trays made of some devious plastic that defied looking clean. The trays had to be thoroughly washed and dried by hand after each use; otherwise they looked grimy.

I was ready to go home at 11:00. I had never had a job that lasted more than a couple hours at a time. I didn't realize two hours could drag so much. We ate lunch at 11:00 because the cafeteria opened at 11:30 and the races started at 2:00. Our lunch choices, spaghetti, meat loaf, or roast beef sandwiches, were actually pretty good for cafeteria food, and my spirits lifted somewhat, but then the real work began.

Once the cafeteria opened we cleaned the dirty dishes off the tables and put them into metal dish carriers, wiped off the tables, separated the silverware and paper from the dishes, and pushed

Waterford Park Racetrack, c. 1950s. (Photo courtesy of the Mountaineer Casino Racetrack & Resort)

the dishes and silverware through the window to the dishwasher. We took the trays to the dirty tray pile. This was the first glitch in the system. None of us wanted to get stuck cleaning the evil trays. Eventually we decided to have two of us bus while the other wrestled with the trays, and then change off every hour. I was exhausted when the cafeteria closed at 5:00. The cafeteria women got to go home, but we had to stay and put the chairs up on the tables and mop the floor. That didn't seem fair and certainly not worth the ninety cents we would get for an hour of floor mopping.

At the end of the day we split $1.10 in tips. The day had lasted an eternity, but it was over and I had lived through it. On the ride home I realized I had to do it again the next day and then again for the next six weeks. I wanted to cry, but because Chuck and Jon were there, I just sat and stared out the window, watching my childhood pass before my eyes.

I did not feel any better when I got home and found that Larry and Bill had slept until 10:00, played baseball, and flirted with girls. The next day they were going swimming at Lake Marwin with a bunch of other kids. That day I learned two important lessons about working. The first was it was long and boring, and the second was what good was money if you didn't have time to spend it?

As the summer progressed, the weather got hotter, making it more difficult to sleep at night. Like most people in Newell, my family did not have air conditioning. Getting up at 7:30 to catch my 8:30 ride was painful. Larry Hutton, who could always emerge from difficult situations smelling like a rose, got a part-time job pumping gas. He was working only fifteen or twenty hours a week at a job that wasn't too difficult. Then things got worse for me.

As the racing season progressed, the crowds began to decline. Mrs. Zagula, the cafeteria supervisor, called the three busboys together and told us that one of us would have to be laid off. Or one of us could take the recently vacated job of dishwasher. I quickly contemplated the beauty of being laid off and not having to work, but felt being laid off from my first job would label me a failure, a label that might follow me all of my life. For a reason I cannot explain even today, I volunteered to be the new dishwasher. I thought, "How could it be worse than being a busboy?" I was wrong. As I passed through the swinging doors into the steamy kitchen, I stepped into a place that only Dante could have adequately described.

My immediate supervisor was the head dishwasher, Howard, whom I nicknamed Howard the Horrible. He was diminutive, only a little bigger than I was, at something like five-feet, five-inches tall, and wore work pants and a dirty t-shirt. However, his most defining characteristics were that he had only one eye and wore a pirate type patch in public; he was missing several teeth, and he looked like he hadn't shaved for a week. The one-eye thing did not bother me too much; my friend Steve Norris had a missing eye because of a BB gun accident. Mothers in Newell who did not want to give their sons BB guns for Christmas had a real example of someone who had shot his eye out with a BB gun. Steve turned out to be an excellent football player, handsome, and somewhat mysterious when he wore his eye patch. Before he was twenty-one, he had married and divorced two beautiful girls. But while Steve wore his artificial eye most of the time when he was in public, Howard claimed his pirate-type eye patch was too hot to wear during work hours. I could not look him in the eye, and with his missing teeth, watching him eat was not a pretty sight either.

Howard operated the dish-rinsing sprayer and the dishwasher. I washed the pots and pans by hand, and did the finish drying when the glasses, cups, and dishes came out of the washer. The dishwasher's corner of the kitchen was extremely hot and humid compared with the air conditioned cafeteria. It didn't smell very good, particularly late in the afternoon when the garbage can filled up with partially eaten food. I soon realized that by choice I had entered my own personal hell. When the steam that rose from the open dishwashing machine partially cleared, a one-eyed demon peered through to deliver garbled orders.

Howard's directions were not very complete or clear. "Whip the asses, then whip and stalk the sassers," he mumbled over the roar of the dishwasher. The missing teeth made it hard to understand what he was saying, and not looking at him didn't help matters. "Hurt wader clenner on bem pats," he barked, and then berated me for not following his directions. I scalded myself on hot water, was drenched in sweat, and had dishpan hands. The days lasted a lifetime, and the weeks were endless. I longed to be a busboy again in the air conditioning with normal people.

Racing season ended just before two-a-day football practice began. Everyone on the team complained that football was hot and boring and the coach was too demanding. I only smiled. That summer I vowed never again to work as a busboy or dishwasher.

The summer of 1960 was the direct opposite in terms of work.

I got a job again at Waterford Park, but this time I was a messenger for the Mutual Department, which sold and cashed the pari-mutual tickets. Wearing a little green jacket and tie, I worked behind the sellers' and cashiers' windows and carried money from the bank or central money room to the ticket sellers, who sometimes needed change, or to the cashiers, who often needed money after they paid out for winning tickets. I sometimes carried up to $1,500 in money bundles. I had to be careful, because that was more money than I would make in three summers. But we had a triple receipt system in which the banker, messenger, and cashier initialed each transaction and kept a copy of one of the receipts.

I started at about noon and left for the day when all the tickets had been cashed from the last race, which was usually 6:00 or 6:30. I worked six days a week for a total of about thirty-six hours. When more than eight races were run I got overtime pay. My pay was $10 a day but, on the Fourth of July when they ran sixteen races, I got $1.10 for each extra race for a bonanza day of $18.80.

The next summer I got a job as a ware boy at The Homer Laughlin China Company. Because the pottery industry was suffering from competition from Japanese pottery, there had been no summer jobs for high school or college boys in recent years. The summer of 1961 was the first time in years the Homer Laughlin pottery hired two high school boys for the summer. The other boy hired was Ken Cunningham from East Liverpool, the best high school athlete in the area. He was named to the Ohio All-State football and basketball teams and was voted "Mr. Basketball" in the state of Ohio. He had accepted a scholarship to play college basketball at the University of Cincinnati, the defending NCAA champions. Ken was hired because he was a star athlete. I was hired because I had befriended Peter Cartwright, whom I always picked to be on my baseball teams when I was the captain. Peter was the shy, young son of the pottery's personnel director.

I was a ware boy in the glaze section, a real adult man's job despite having boy in the job title. In fact, some of my friends' fathers had the same job that I was now doing. The job paid $1.75 an hour, which was really good for a kid, but not much for

Women inspecting cups on the assembly line at The Homer Laughlin China company, c.1950s. (Photo courtesy of The Homer Laughlin China Company)

a man with a family. That was why many of the mothers of my friends worked in the pottery too; it took two pottery salaries to keep a family going. The women who worked in the glaze section were unskilled line workers. Red-faced and kind of crude, they told off-color jokes when I wasn't around, but got quiet when I came within hearing distance. I did not know any of them or their kids, and they made me a little nervous.

The glaze belt was not a good place to work in the pottery. It was dirty, dusty, and didn't have much light or ventilation. The glaze belts were in the middle of the factory where there were no windows, only skylights that did not let in much light or fresh air. Once in the plant I could not tell if it was sunny or raining. The pottery was not air conditioned so work started at 6:30 a.m., when it was cool, and ended at 3:30 p.m. We had thirty minutes for lunch and two fifteen-minute breaks. For a high school boy who liked going to dances, dating, and playing sports, getting up for work at 5:45 and spending the day in a hot, confined space was torture. On the other hand, I made seventy dollars a week and did not have to work on Saturdays as I had at the racetrack.

The job did not begin well. On the first day the foreman said to me, "Do you know ware?" I responded, "No, where?" After a couple of rounds of this I thought I was in a Bud Abbot and Lou Costello skit, but he was serious. He realized I did not know ware and probably did not know where either. From then on he had to describe the ware he wanted by saying things like, "the little dishes with the ring in the middle" or "the cups with the funny handle." He felt it was demeaning to have to describe the fine ware they were making in those childish terms, but he did what he had to do to keep the production line moving.

Once the foreman told me which kind of ware he wanted, I went to the end of the tunnel kiln where the fired, unglazed pottery came out and picked up a huge rolling rack of rough ware. The ware was arranged on eight-foot long boards that were placed lengthwise on a rack which was taller than I was and about six feet wide. I had to push the rack to the women who worked on the end of the glaze conveyor belt, and place the boards of ware next to the conveyor belt. The women would lift the ware off the boards and place it on the conveyor belt to be sprayed with liquid glaze before being fired again. This seems difficult to screw up, but I managed. I could not see around the racks and was impatient to boot, I tended to run into things, like the columns that held up the roof. This caused the boards to fall off of the racks. Once the rack got out of control, there was no way I could stop it. Broken dishes lay all along the path from the tunnel kiln to the glaze belt. The foreman would just look at them and shake his head. The women would giggle.

After a week of failure as a ware boy in the glaze shop, Mr. Cartwright, the personnel director, came to speak with me. He decided that rather than fire me, he would transfer me to the decorating shop, where they decorated the dishes or ware before the final firing. The decorating shop was located in a huge corner room with giant opaque windows, so there was plenty of light. The area was clean, because they did not want to get imperfections on the ware before the final firing.

Although a semi-skilled position, work as a decorator was one of the highest paid jobs for women in the pottery. The job required a precise touch. On one production line, gold lines were painted on the rims of white saucers. In another section, decals were taken from a sheet of decals and placed on the center of dishes. The women who worked on the decal line were paid by how many pieces of decorated ware they turned out in a day. Their hands worked in a blur as they unerringly put decal after decal on the exact centers of the dishes. The women, many of them the mothers of my friends, were much more polite than the glaze belt women, but they did not have time to stop and talk, particularly if they were on piecework. My job was somewhat easier because the ware was stacked in bins, which I easily moved by using a jack on wheels.

Though the decorating shop was an easier and more pleasant place to work, I still had to get up early in the morning and work a full eight hours, leaving me tired at the end of the day. I was glad to see the summer end so I could start college in the fall.

———

I learned two very important lessons from these work experiences. One lesson was that a lot of people, including some of my friends' parents, had difficult jobs that paid little, and their work conditions were never going to improve. The second lesson was that going to college was much easier. Whenever things got tough in college, like having two tests on a day when I was hung over, I motivated myself by saying, "I could be working in the pottery pushing a ware truck with this hangover." In fact, the memory of my jobs in the pottery and as a dishwasher frightened me so badly I worked through three college degrees.

The 1959 Sadie Hawkins Dance, a girl-ask-boy dance, where everyone dressed up like the hillbilly characters from the *Li'l Abner* comic strip. My date, Denise Bowen, is on the far right. (Photo from the 1960 Newell High School Yearbook courtesy of Ruth and Joe Fuller)

Chapter 12

Love, Sex, and Dances

Love began early in Newell. I was attracted to my first girlfriend, Denise Bowen, in fourth grade because she had a pony cart. I don't remember what the pony looked like, but his name was Tony. Denise had straight brown hair which she wore in braids until she was in high school. With brown eyes and a husky voice, she bore a faint resemblance to Princess Summerfall Winterspring on the *Howdy Doody Show*. Like every other little boy in America I loved the Princess.

Newell was so small that Denise's parents were able to stable a pony in the middle of town. Traffic was so light that when they hitched the pony to its cart, Denise's parents felt safe in allowing a ten-year-old to drive it wherever she wanted to go. On a number of occasions, she drove her pony cart down Washington Street and then up Grant Street to my house so that she could take me for a ride. The other boys teased me about riding with a girl, but I didn't care. I was the one riding in the cart.

I became even more interested in Denise in the fall of eighth grade when she asked me to the Sadie Hawkins Dance, a girl-ask-boy dance where everyone dressed up like the hillbilly characters from the *Li'l Abner* comic strip. Like all the girls, Denise dressed up as Daisy Mae in a polka dot, low cut blouse and a black, very short skirt. She looked much different, but I couldn't quite figure out what was so different about her.

When I took her to the Christmas Dance a couple of months later, I noticed how her pigtails flowed over the tight, tiger print dress she wore. I realized then that she had breasts and a budding woman's body. I was so excited by the discovery that I held hands with her under the table, to my friends' surprise. She made my hormones start to flow and I did not even know what hormones were.

After the dance we walked back to her house holding hands. When we arrived, her mother was sitting in the living room watching television. Denise and I sat side by side on a couch behind her. Soon we were engaged in some heavy eighth-grade kissing. Mrs. Bowen's chair was close to the TV and her back was toward us; she never turned or seemed to notice our activities. I thought we were home free.

Unfortunately, we were not. On Monday, Denise told me her mother had seen our reflection in the window and later gave her a long lecture on what to do and not to do with boys. Mrs. Bowen regarded me with suspicion from then on and was never very friendly toward me. She was the first of many mothers who seemed to read my mind. I was never sure whether my motives were so transparent that those mothers could see right through me, or if they distrusted every boy who showed an interest in their daughters.

Recently, I asked my friend Corey Lock if he and his wife Grace ever went anywhere to dance. Corey was shocked at the question; "Why would I do that? I have never danced since the day I got married. I only went to dances to meet girls. Now that I'm married

I don't have to go through the mating ritual anymore." A veil was lifted from my eyes; his comment was so clear and insightful that I almost cried. Yes, it was a mating ritual; I had gone to dances to try to find a girl to mate with, something I hoped would occur right after each dance.

Rituals, one of the most enduring parts of any culture, can mark the passage of time or the passage from one phase of life to another. Though celebrating change, these rituals provide a sense of stability and comfort by affirming that change is expected and appropriate. The rituals are vehicles to pass down the beliefs and values of a society from one generation to another. Mating rituals not only reflect the values of the society but also serve to regenerate the tribe. In Newell in the 1950s and early 1960s, the cornerstone of the mating ritual was the high school dance.

In the fifties, no one would have been so forthright as to label high school dances mating rituals. Instead, adults talked about the importance of extracurricular activities to prevent juvenile delinquency. Like most of the country, Newell was terror-stricken by the fear that bored teenagers would drive fast cars, vandalize, join gangs, and get into rumbles. The fear had been touched off by the publication of *Blackboard Jungle* in 1954, and when *The Ladies Home Journal* published a special condensed edition of the book that was followed by a movie version, all America could see how juvenile delinquency was destroying its schools. When *Rebel Without a Cause* was released in 1955, James Dean convinced adults that juvenile delinquency was a nationwide epidemic. To combat this epidemic, Newell and Chester held dances. It must have worked, because although we were often threatened with reform school in Pruntytown, home to the West Virginia Boys' Industrial School, I don't remember kids doing anything more serious than having a loud muffler or driving too fast. We'll never know whether we would have avoided reform school without dances, but it's clear that we spent much of our time and energy dancing.

Six major high school dances were held each year in Newell during the 1950s and early 1960s. The format of the dance and the month it was held were set in stone.

The high school dance season started in late September with the Sadie Hawkins dance. We were allowed to attend this dance while in the seventh grade. At that point, we did not have any idea about how to invite each other, and six different girls asked me to the dance. I was not the only boy this happened to. Our parents told us we could not wait to see who asked us, but we had to go with the first girl who asked or not go to the dance at all. For the next dance, the boys asked the girls and we were better at spreading the word through an informal grapevine about who was still available.

For the Sadie Hawkins dance and every other school dance, a queen and court were named, usually seniors. This was one of the few opportunities that girls had to be recognized other than academics and music (girls' sports being limited at this time). In Newell there was a long standing tradition that we picked a different queen and court for almost every dance. At some high schools the prettiest girl got to be queen of everything; but in Newell the honors were spread around. With only seventeen girls in my class, by the time the prom rolled around at the end of the year, almost every girl had her night to shine. Doesn't everyone need to be queen or at least princess for a day?

The next two dances were the homecoming dance and the Christmas dance. These were boy-ask-girl, unless the girl wanted to ask someone from another school. Those were semiformal dances where the boys wore either sport coats or suits and ties and the girls wore nice dresses and heels.

The Homecoming Dance was part of our homecoming celebration that began with a parade on Thursday followed by the

The 1956 Homecoming Parade. Seated left to right in the Buick convertible are Judy Jackson, Brenda Staley, Karen Broomhall, and Judy Anderson. (Photo from the 1957 Newell High School Yearbook)

football game on Friday and culminated with the dance on Saturday. The homecoming parade was very small. The football team, riding on Newell's fire truck, led the parade. I loved riding the fire truck as a football player. We wore our game jerseys and waved to people as the fire siren blew. When the parade went past my house, my family was always out on the porch cheering. The team was followed by convertibles carrying the candidates for homecoming queen. Each girl sat on the top of the back seat of an open convertible with her name written on poster boards taped to the sides of the car. The Newell High School band brought up the end of the parade. Riding in this parade, small though it was, ranked as a high point in life.

The homecoming football game drew more fans than an average game because many people came to see the homecoming queen crowned at halftime. Although Newell alumni never traveled from long distances for homecoming, almost everyone in town felt they were a part of the tradition. Many of the adults had played football and ridden the fire truck or marched in the homecoming parade in what seemed only a short time before. Now they wanted to watch the next generation, most of whom they knew well, participate in the same ritual. The Homecoming Dance was almost anticlimactic after the excitement of the parade and game.

The Christmas Dance my senior year was memorable because I took Pam Rockwell, from Chester, who I was dating at the time. Pam was short and a little chubby. The guys teased me when they found out I was dating her. Jake Geer was particularly cutting when he said, "Pam is not a dish; she's more like the whole bowl." I began to wonder if I should continue with her, but then remembered she was actually very cute and had a great sense of humor. We were convulsed in laughter most of the time on our dates. I had to be careful drinking Coca-Cola when I was with her because she often made me laugh so hard the Coke came out of my nose.

When I went to pick her up the night of the Christmas Dance, she was wearing high heels, which made her look taller and more graceful, and, as my eyes ran up her clingy dress, I realized she looked voluptuous. Her waist was thin and her breasts were large; the term "hourglass figure" fit her perfectly. I was speechless, but Ronnie Moffitt, who was double-dating with us, and much more articulate, could not suppress a "wow" when I helped Pam off with her coat.

All through the dance, guys kept coming up to me to talk; even guys I barely knew acted as if we were long lost friends. Some of them angled for an introduction to Pam. Most of them, including Jake Geer, knew her already, but either didn't recognize her or just wanted an excuse to get a closer look.

I am not sure what magic formula brought about the change in Pam's appearance, but I suspect it was some kind of a long line

Pam "Wow" Rockwell and I posing at the 1960 Christmas Dance. (Photo by Ronnie Moffitt)

girdle with a push up bra. It must have been painful for Pam to wear or she may have used it only for special occasions, because I never saw her in that outfit again. I guess I should have learned from that experience how superficial and fleeting physical attractiveness and a big chest were, but like most other guys I had to be taught that lesson over and over again.

The second half of the school year featured the Sweetheart Prom and the Band Dance. The Sweetheart Prom, a Valentine's Day girl-ask-boy dance, gave the girls a chance to wear their prom dresses from the previous year. For the boys, it meant a chance to see real live cleavage. Of course we tried not to stare, but we did. This cleavage was not on a movie screen or in a dirty magazine; it was right there, pushing against our chests.

The Band Dance was usually held in late April or early May. The band parents held a banquet for band members, and then a dance to which the kids in the band could bring a date. This dance was one of the last chances for someone to find a date for the prom.

During the spring of my senior year I had been dating Jennifer Allison, the sister of my hero, Jim Allison, who twice had stolen my girlfriend, Carolyn Brenneman, from me. Jennifer asked me to go to the Band Dance with her three weeks before the dance. By the week of the dance I was more interested in going to Hi-Teen to see Liz Arner, who I had begun dating in the meantime. But it was bad manners to break a date, and I still kind of liked Jennifer, so I went to the Band Dance. Because of the code, neither Liz nor I said anything about it to each other.

Adolescent love hinged on some strange things. Jennifer was almost as tall as me, and when we slow danced her body fit nicely with mine. But at this more formal dance, she wore heels, and we did not fit together as well. Our relationship was over, simple as that.

I never realized just how many of our high school dances were "girl-ask-boy." When I mentioned this to Liz recently, she looked at me as if I were stupid and said, "Of course, high school was where a lot of girls would find their husbands and the women teachers wanted to help the process along." In that sense, Newell was way ahead of women's lib.

The last dance of the school year was the prom. As the most important social event on the high school social schedule, the prom deserves a chapter of its own, which follows this one.

⌣

Dances were so popular we went to a dance every week or even twice a week if we went to Hi-Teen in Chester. Those dances were the high point of the week once we got into high school. We could go to the dances after every Friday home football and basketball game and on Saturday night to Hi-Teen. We went to these dances stag unless we were going steady.

In the '50s, we had a precise lexicon of terms to describe the various stages of the mating ritual. "Going steady" meant you were in an exclusive dating relationship. Some couples went steady for years. Ruth McCabe and Joe Fuller, a tackle on the football team, went steady during their senior year until they were married in 1966. Others were more like Harp McCune, another football player, who would always be going steady with a new girl within a week of a breakup. I have no idea how Harp lined them up so fast. My parents, like many others, worried that going steady would lead to too much intimacy and eventually to wild sex. I was never that lucky with the three girls I went steady with in high school.

Couples who were not going steady but who had had more than two dates were described as "dating." It was considered bad form for girls to flirt with boys their friends were dating. It was a less serious breach of etiquette for boys to ask out someone who was dating another boy than to ask out someone who was going steady, but both could lead to fistfights, although few rumbles occurred over these breaches. Another relationship level was "going out," which denoted a short-term or sporadic relationship. Understanding the terminology was essential in order to know who could be asked to dance.

On Fridays we crowded the high school gym for low-key, after-game dances sponsored by the cheerleaders. Students played records with no disc jockey patter between songs, and the only special effect was dimming the overhead lights. These dances were the dreaded sock hops. Everyone took off their shoes because the basketball coaches thought dancing in shoes on the gym floor would leave black marks or scratch its pristine surface. Some coaches were so worried about their floors that nobody was allowed on the gym floor in street shoes except the coaches during a game. The danger of a scratched surface was possible, because some boys wore metal covers on the heels of their shoes to keep them from wearing down. I never saw any black marks or scratches on gym floors that were caused by dances.

I hated sock hops because they ruined the cool white socks that I, like most of the boys, wore. Besides, as I danced my feet felt clammy and gritty as if there were dirt between my toes. It was just as bad for the girls who either got their white bobby socks impossibly dirty or ruined a pair of hose. However, even the dreaded sock hop did not deter me or anyone else from participating in these high school mating rituals.

Hi-Teen, a dance held in the small gym above Chester's city hall, was never a sock hop because there were no basketball coaches to worry about the floor there. The gym floor was very rough to begin with, and part of it was covered with a sea of gum discarded by hundreds of gum chewing adolescents and ground into the wood grain as they danced. The gum turned black as it picked up dirt. At first the city hall janitor tried to scrape up the gum, but the more he tried the more gum that appeared, almost like an amoeba multiplying. Eventually he gave up and just let the gum pile grow. The court was used only occasionally for basketball, but during those games when the lights were on we saw that the gum covered about a third of the court off to the side where the midcourt line intersected with the out of bounds line. This was where the largest group of stag girls stood at Hi-Teen. The basketball lines were so obliterated by the gum that we could only guess at the court boundaries. I thought it might be difficult to dribble the ball over the gum, but surprisingly the gum had solidified and was as hard as the floor. It didn't seem much different from the rest of the floor, although no one wanted to fall down in that area.

Hi-Teen was held every Saturday night and also on Wednesday nights during the summer. Bermuda shorts were allowed on Wednesday, but on Saturday the boys wore slacks and the girls wore dresses or skirts and blouses. Even though Chester and Newell were athletic rivals, the Hi-Teen dance provided an opportunity for us to interact socially, and Newell and Chester kids became great friends. In fact, I had almost as many friends from Chester as I did from Newell and eventually married a Chester girl.

I am not sure who was the official sponsor of Hi-Teen, but Mrs. Hindes (pronounced Hinds), my friend Tom's mother, and Mrs. Miller, mother of Susie Miller, another friend, were the chaperones. Mrs. Miller guarded the door and took our twenty-five-cent admission. Mrs. Hindes and Mrs. Miller were paid five dollars each night, with the excess money from admissions going for new records. Both women provided a great service by giving their time for very little money, and we kids liked and respected them for what they did. In 2009 they were honored with induction into the Chester Hall of Fame for their seventeen years of service to the kids of Chester.

The Hi-Teen dances followed the same pattern each week. The gym became a dance floor when the lights were turned very low. We became shadowy figures, somewhat mysterious, and immediately more attractive because the dim light hid pimples, bad haircuts, and other imperfections that haunt teenagers in the light. The smell also had an erotic quality. All the girls wore perfume that often conflicted with the extreme amount of hair spray used to keep their '50s hairstyles in place. Sometimes boys got stuck to the girls' hair when they slow danced. And the boys wore way too much aftershave lotion. Aqua Velva and Old Spice were the most popular, even though few of us shaved more than once a month. Strangely, the heavy smells blended with adolescent sweat only superficially covered up by Mum or Arrid deodorant to form an erotic, musky smell. The smell was so pungent we could hear male dogs howling for blocks around when the gym door was opened.

Lucky to be teenagers coming of age when rock and roll was gathering steam, we were in that period between the Beatles and Perry Como, a popular Italian crooner who still cranked out number one hits in 1957 like "Round and Round" and "Catch a Falling Star." By the late 1950s, teenage music had taken over the music industry. In that golden age the music ranged from romantic ballads to fast moving rock-and-roll songs backed by loud electric guitars or novelty songs with silly lyrics. The music spoke to us as nothing had before, because it was ours. Our parents hated it, which made us like it even more.

Mrs. Hindes played the Top 40 hits without commentary, except to occasionally announce a ladies' choice dance. A shrewd DJ who knew her audience, she would begin by playing some novelty songs such as "The Lion Sleeps Tonight":

> In the jungle, the mighty jungle
> The lion sleeps tonight
> Wimoweh Wimoweh Wimoweh Wimoweh
> > (The Tokens, 1961)

She would then throw in some up-tempo songs like "At The Hop," a number one hit by Danny and the Juniors in 1958:

> Well, you can rock it you can roll it
> You can stomp and you can stroll it at the hop.

Girls would jitterbug with each other to those songs, but most of the guys were too shy to jitterbug to fast dances.

After a couple warm-up songs, Mrs. Hindes would play some

slow songs to see if the boys were ready to start asking girls to dance. Boys were often reluctant to begin the dancing. But Mrs. Hindes would begin to throw in more slow songs and suddenly announce, "Ladies' choice." The girls were not as shy as the boys about getting things going. For the first ladies' choice, she would play something like Elvis' "Love Me Tender":

> Love me tender
> Love me true
> All my dreams fulfilled.
>
> (Elvis Presley, 1956)

As the evening progressed, Mrs. Hindes mixed slow and fast songs and ladies' choices. After awhile, the boys were not as shy about asking the girls to dance. When we recognized the song was going to be a slow one, like "The Magic Touch," we would move toward the crowd of girls standing together, on the gum spot. Taking someone's elbow I would suavely ask, "Would you like to dance?" As the Platters crooned, "You've got the magic touch/It makes me glow so much" (The Platters, 1956), I would pull her close. The scent of her perfume, the feel of her body rhythmically moving against mine, and the slow suggestive music made me feel one with the Platters' song. It was enough to make a teenage boy's heart pound out of control.

Often, couples dating or going steady stood together along the wall or windows. Sometimes they became overcome by the moment and kissed passionately. At those times Mrs. Miller immediately went over and told them to cool down or she would have to ask them to leave. I don't remember her sending anyone home, but there were times when she had to speak to the same couple twice during the evening.

The last six dances included at least two ladies' choice dances.

Mrs. Hindes strategically placed them toward the end of the evening so that the boys could see if the girls they had been asking to dance were interested in being taken home by them, or the girls could demonstrate their interest in being taken home.

After I had staked out the girl I wanted to take home, I would ask her to dance. Usually the next to last song was a romantic ballad like the classic "Unchained Melody." As Al Hibbler sang, "Lonely rivers flow to the sea, to the sea, to the open arms of the sea," I would ask to take her home. If she accepted, we would stand together, arm in arm, waiting for the next song. A favorite last song was Johnny Mathis' "The Twelfth of Never."

> Hold me close and never let me go
> Hold me close; melt my heart like April snow
> I'll love you till bluebells forget to bloom...
> Until the twelfth of never, and that's a long, long time.
> (Johnny Mathis, 1957)

I met my future wife, Liz Arner, who lived in Chester, after Hi-Teen on New Year's Eve, 1960. I had been dating Pam Rockwell, Liz's best friend, and that evening I asked if I could walk Pam home, because I did not have the car, and Pam lived only two blocks from Hi-Teen. To my surprise, Pam was going to a slumber party at Liz's house that night, so I walked her there and she introduced me to Liz. I remember thinking, "Liz is really cute, has a good sense of humor, is quite interesting and very sexy looking." For the next three months, I looked for her at Hi-Teen every week and at the dances after basketball games, but she never appeared. It was almost as if she were a ghost; her memory haunted me.

Then on the Saturday before Easter, Liz came to Hi-Teen. Both of us were in groups of stag boys and girls. I asked her to dance a couple of times and she asked me on the second ladies'

choice. Later, Liz said she did not like me initially because of the impersonal way she thought I had treated Pam, but then when we started to dance she liked the soft red shirt I was wearing and became more interested the more we danced. I asked her to dance frequently that night and we asked each other during the crucial last six dances of the evening.

When I asked to take her home, she agreed. With two other couples, we drove to Hoge's, a drive-in restaurant in back of East Liverpool. At Hoge's, everybody always ordered a hamburger and chocolate milkshake, almost as if it were an unwritten rule. I was astounded when Liz ordered a Shrub, which I learned was grape juice with ice cream. As I sat there with my hamburger and chocolate milkshake, I realized that Liz was something special to break tradition in such a bold way.

Shrub-drinking Liz Arner—"really cute, has a good sense of humor, and very sexy looking"—with her future husband. Rock Springs Park summer 1961.

Liz Arner and Bob Barnett at the 1961 prom, The Most Wonderful Night of Their Lives.

Chapter 13
The Prom

The high point of the high school social scene was the annual Junior-Senior Prom which we expected to be "the most wonderful night of our life." In Newell we could go to the prom in our junior and senior years. However, if we could dance, cleaned up presentably, and had decent manners, we could attend even more proms. I attended four of them. When I was a sophomore, I was asked to the prom by my steady girlfriend, a junior; as a senior, I was asked to the Chester High School Prom by Liz Arner, my steady girlfriend at that time. And, of course, I attended my own junior and senior proms. For me, each of the four actually was the most wonderful night of my life.

In Newell and other small towns in the 1950s, proms were a rite of passage into adulthood. While tests and term papers prepared us for graduation and the opportunity to work in the real world, sock hops, Hi-Teen, and school dances prepared us for the prom—the one dazzling, all-night final exam where we could demonstrate our social skills and readiness to move on to adult social events.

Ironically, no adult event ever approached the grandeur and

excitement of a high school prom. Although many college dances, country club events, and New Year's Eve parties make feeble attempts to equal a prom, most of those events turn out to be disappointing. Even adults in Newell appreciated the importance of the prom; it had been either the most wonderful night of their own lives, or a source of lasting envy and shame for those who missed it.

———

The prom consumed our lives for months. Right after Christmas vacation, the junior class was divided into the decorating committee, the orchestra committee, the refreshments committee, and the fundraising committee. The committees met endlessly to consider every possible idea and detail. For us, these were crucial, life-defining decisions. In fact, they were too important to be left up to the committees alone; the class as a whole had to vote on every recommendation.

I was appointed to the all-important fundraising committee. We had to raise all the money to pay for the prom, because we did not charge admission or sell tickets. Without enough money, we would be faced with the prospect of playing records instead of having an orchestra and serving Kool-Aid instead of punch and cookies. We estimated it would take more than $400 to pay for the decorations, orchestra, and refreshments.

We were not very creative fundraisers. After much debate we decided to do exactly what the classes before us had done. In February and March, we sold valentines and held raffles and bake sales. We were not very good at any of those. As spring approached, we realized the prom was getting closer and closer and we had not raised much money. Would we be remembered as the class that ruined the prom? The sight of Kool-Aid at dinner began to make me nervous. We knew the success of our fundraising efforts and the reputation of our class hinged on one event, the annual junior class spaghetti dinner.

Spaghetti dinners, popular fundraising events in Newell, were held two or three times every year by churches and clubs. The labor was free, stores in town often gave the sponsoring groups a discount on the food, and spaghetti was a popular dish. It was an exotic food for families like mine. Some of the women in town used Chef Boy-Ar-Dee spaghetti sauce, but not my mother. She felt the Chef Boy-Ar-Dee brand was too spicy and only the lazy used canned sauce. Mom made her own wonderful spaghetti, using liberal amounts of sugar to make up for the lack of other spices in the tomato sauce. Mom believed any time tomatoes were in a recipe, sugar belonged there too; she used the same approach for her homemade chili, which consisted of sweetened tomato soup with hamburger and kidney beans. I loved her spaghetti, and chili too for that matter, until I tasted the rich, red, spicy sauce and melt-in-your-mouth meatballs served at the Naples Restaurant and the Roma Café across the river in East Liverpool. I was immediately hooked on Italian spaghetti and couldn't wait for a chance for more. I felt better about fundraising just thinking about a spaghetti dinner.

Newell had a large Italian population with women who really knew how to make spaghetti and meatballs. Unfortunately, there were no Italians in my class. When the junior class mothers got together to plan the cooking, they realized that no one knew how to make real Italian spaghetti sauce, to say nothing of meatballs. This was a disaster. The sauce was important, but the meatballs were a big part of what made the spaghetti dinners in Newell so good. Two large, round succulent meatballs were placed on every plate of spaghetti at the fundraisers. If an organization could not promise sauce and meatballs made by one of the great Italian cooks in town, few tickets would be sold. On the other hand, if they could promise food made by Mrs. Raimond, the queen of meatballs, the tickets would sell themselves.

Even the older Italian women in town who had been born in Italy recognized Mrs. Raimond's meatballs as the best in Newell, and she was asked to help make the meatballs at every spaghetti dinner held in Newell. Mrs. Raimond, her husband, and their three sons lived in a house on Washington Street, the first floor of which had been their shoe repair shop before they moved the business to East Liverpool. Her son Bob was a year younger than we were but a good friend of mine. Even though Bob, at 5'4" and very slow, was without question one of the worst basketball players ever to attend Newell High School, no one ever made fun of him. He was really cool in the kind of mature way that Italian boys had about them in the 1950s. Plus, we always hoped he might share some of his mother's meatballs.

Mrs. Raimond's meatballs were a blend of hamburger, spice, and bread crumbs that were a pure delight when covered with marinara sauce. They were firm enough to hold their roundness until they were on the plate, but when touched by a fork they magically broke into very edible halves and quarters. Mom had worked on the meatball crew with Mrs. Raimond for a couple of fundraisers and claimed the secret was in the bread crumbs that Mrs. Raimond mixed with the ground beef. But when Mom tried to replicate the meatballs, they tasted like plain hamburger and either had the consistency of golf balls or fell apart in the sauce.

Mrs. Raimond was in such demand that she was getting tired of making forty dozen meatballs two or three times a year for spaghetti dinners. Since she had no children in our class, she might very well say no to helping us. But we had a secret weapon, my Mom. The Raimonds were one of the few Italian families who were not Roman Catholics. They attended the same Presbyterian Church my family did. My mother made an emergency phone call to her.

Begging and pleading, Mom talked her into agreeing to coming to the fire station to supervise making the sauce and meatballs for the dinner.

The most important part of the success of any spaghetti dinner was to sell tickets in advance, because an advance sale meant you had the money whether people came to the dinner or not. At two dollars a ticket, the dinner wasn't cheap. However, when we went out to sell tickets, we were able to say, "Mrs. Raimond will be in charge of the meatballs." That helped. Everyone came through for us. Mom sold twenty tickets at her job at the racetrack, mostly to people who owed her because she had bought tickets from them in the past. I sold eighteen going door-to-door on Grant Street. Larry Hutton's mother sold twenty-five tickets to coworkers and Bill Moffitt sold twenty tickets to the customers on his newspaper route. Everyone in the class got out and hustled, because we knew our backs were to the wall. All thirty-four members of our class sold multiple tickets.

The dinner took place on a beautiful, warm April day. We sold more tickets at the door and the firemen's hall was packed. Margaret Donovan, Mary Huff, and Marlene Daugherty led the girls in the class in serving the plates of spaghetti our moms had dished up. I headed up the dishwashing crew, because I had been a professional dishwasher at the racetrack. Frank Gilmore, Eugene Hart, and Gary Evans bussed the tables. No one messed around because there was too much work to do. At 8:00 we closed the door and again everyone pitched in to clear the tables and set them up for the firemen's bingo the next night.

The dinner was a huge success. Not only was the food good, but everyone shared the work. We cleared over $400, making more than enough money to pay for the prom in style. As we finished the cleanup, I looked around at my classmates and had a new appreciation for the kids I had gone to school with for almost eleven years. Never before had I seen such a seriousness of purpose, a loyalty to each other, and a willingness to work together.

⟵

The most important pre-prom activity began in mid-April, when it was time to begin thinking about a date for the prom. This was not to be taken lightly, because everyone wanted to go to the prom and everyone wanted it to be the most wonderful night of their lives. Having the right date was really important.

Fortunately, I never had to worry about a prom date because I was going steady with Carolyn Brenneman during prom my junior year and with Liz Arner during my senior year, so I could watch with some detachment. But for the kids who needed to find a date, the process was extremely tense.

There were a number of unwritten rules and a time line for asking a date. Failure to follow them branded the rule violator for the rest of his or her life as the boob who did not know proper prom etiquette. All the junior and senior class was invited. This gave both boys and girls an opportunity to ask someone to go with them, so asking was not just a male prerogative. However, it was not proper for a junior or senior girl to ask a junior or senior boy; she had to wait to be asked by them, but she was free to ask a sophomore or freshman boy or someone who did not go to Newell High School.

The most important rule of prom invitation was that you had to go with the first person who asked you, or not go at all. It was an unacceptable breach of etiquette to wait to see who would ask you and then pick one. We had learned this rule in the seventh grade, when the same person was asked to a dance by a number of people and feelings were hurt. This rule may have seemed like an invitation to disaster because if the wrong person asked you the prom could turn into the most *awful* night of your life. Built into the system were numerous folkways and unwritten sub-rules that for the most part kept this from happening and most people got the best date possible.

There were two ways to avoid "first person-asking" problems. The first was to go out on a date with the person you were considering asking to the prom to test your compatibility and his or her level of interest in going to the prom with you. The second way was to use the grapevine to find out who was interested in going with you. The grapevine usually consisted of a couple girls who kept up with all the relationships in the school. Judy Jackson, a year ahead of me in school, was the best matchmaker in Newell. Judy, one of the coolest girls in Newell, knew all of the latest dance steps because she was an avid fan of *American Bandstand*, the televised dance program hosted by Dick Clark that came out of south Philadelphia at 4:00 every weekday afternoon. Judy was so in tune with the show that she not only knew all the hot new dances and songs, but she even knew who was dating whom on the show.

In Newell she was always on top of breaking news like who was dating whom, and in many instances she was so far ahead of the curve she knew in advance who was about to break up or start going steady or even be asked out on a date by a mysterious stranger.

This matchmaker system was what made the prom work. Almost everyone realized they should get Judy's opinion about who they should ask to the prom. Judy was so good that in many cases she had intuitively matched them up already, had checked with the person to be asked, and knew whether the potential date was interested. Otherwise she would ask, "If so-and-so would ask you to the prom would you go?" Occasionally she would even prompt a shy junior or senior by saying, "I know who wants to go to the prom with you." Often this would be enough to set the wheels in motion. Although this system seems a little brash and

Judy Jackson, the Newell Prom matchmaker. (Photo from the 1958 Newell High School Yearbook)

direct, to Judy's credit almost everyone who wanted to go to the prom had a date with very few mismatches.

There were a few times, however, when this system broke down. In 1959, five weeks before the prom, out of the blue, Russell Fetty asked Carol Nease to the prom. Asking Carol without warning was not the only impetuous thing that Russell ever did; he also almost killed me.

Russell was the son of a Nazarene minister, but he was always around trouble. Most ministers' sons I knew were either wild and crazy or very quiet and religious. There did not seem to be an in-between. Russell was known for being wild, impulsive, telling tall tales, chasing girls, and driving too fast. He never was in trouble but if trouble was around he would be close; he lived on the edge.

My near-death experience came following football practice on an August evening in 1958. After football practice, Coach Horoszko gave us our game jerseys so we could wear them the next day when we went out to sell advertisements for the game programs. We all immediately put the jerseys on, saying we wanted to try them on for size, but we really wanted to show them off. We decided the best place to do that would be at the Hookstown Fair, about fifteen miles away just across the state line in Pennsylvania. We did not have enough cars for everybody who wanted to go, so six of us climbed into the back of Russell's pickup truck, where we stood up and held on to the pipe rack.

The ride to the fair was exhilarating. Riding in the back of a pickup truck, on a late summer evening, with my teammates, wearing my football jersey and waving to people as we drove through Newell and Chester was as good as life gets.

Driving out of Chester toward Hookstown on US Route 30, a hilly, twisty two-lane road was also exciting. Russell put the pedal to the metal. We hit fifty or sixty miles per hour going downhill and the tires squealed going around the tight bends in the road. The wind blowing through my flattop, which I kept cut short to be cool for football practice, gave me a tingly feeling, and I felt a sense of speed, freedom, and adventure. But when we crossed the state line into Pennsylvania we got behind a slow truck on a blind curve. Without slowing down, Russell pulled into the other lane only to see a car approaching in that lane. We screamed from the back of the truck, horns honked, and tires screeched. Two trucks and a car squeezed into a two-lane road. Miraculously we slipped between the car and truck. Safely back in our lane, Russell laughed a high-pitched, insane laugh and yelled over the rushing wind, "That was pretty close, huh?" No one in the back of the truck answered or spoke for the rest of the trip. We exchanged looks that said, "We should pinch ourselves to see if we are still alive."

It was the same kind of recklessness that led Russell to ask Carol Nease to go to the prom five weeks in advance. Carol was not impressed with Russell. "I did not want to go to the prom with Russell. I wanted to go with someone else. So I asked my mom what to do," Carol Nease Stomieroski told me recently. "Mom said you have to go with Russell or not go to the prom at all. The next day I told him I would go with him."

During the five long weeks between Russell's invitation and the prom, Carol and Harp McCune fell deeply in love. Tragically, Carol and Harp could not go to the prom together because Russell had not followed prom etiquette. Harp went to the prom with another girl. The week after the prom Carol and Harp McCune were going steady. That experience should have taught Russell a lesson, but of course it did not. A couple years later he was involved in a traffic fatality. He told me he was driving on West Virginia Route 2 south of Wellsburg, West Virginia, when a man who had been drinking heavily staggered out of a roadside bar directly into the path of his car, and was killed instantly. Though the police did not cite Russell, I could tell he was shaken up by the experience.

The second most important rule of prom invitation etiquette was that people who were going steady should go to the prom together. Although the two assumed they would go together, a formal invitation was necessary. The appropriate time for the formal asking was one month before the prom.

There were occasional exceptions to the going steady rule. The classic example occurred in the spring of 1961, a month before the prom, when Mr. Russell "Chisel Chin" Slack, the principal of

Jennifer Thornberry was a very precocious and attractive girl, but even so an eighth grader would not ordinarily have the maturity to attract and keep a senior boy interested. But most eighth graders did not have mothers like Jennifer's. Jean Thornberry devoted her life to coaching Jennifer and her younger sisters, Jill and Jody, on how to attract boys. Jean Thornberry was an interesting character, so interesting she was later the subject of a book written by Jennifer's daughter, Allison Glock, in 2003. The book, *Beauty Before Comfort: A Memoir*, was one of the few published books actually set, for the most part, in Newell.

I did not know Mrs. Thornberry very well, but I certainly heard a lot about her from Bill over the next two years while he was going steady with Jennifer. Mrs. Thornberry was a very attractive woman, although nothing extraordinary. She bragged to Bill she could have been in movies or had an acting career on stage, but she did not have the chance because she was living in Newell. Despite her claims of show business potential, she never displayed any talent for singing or acting that I ever saw. She was never in any of the talent shows or plays that were put on in the area, and she did not even sing in the church choir. She was a stay-at-home mom, not active in any of the community clubs or activities, and Bill said Mr. Thornberry had to do a lot of the cooking after he came home from the grocery store he owned.

Mrs. Thornberry did focus her energy on teaching the tricks of dating to her daughters. Jennifer was her first pupil and pulling the boy on top while falling was one of her first successful lessons. Mrs. Thornberry was in her glory when her daughters brought their boyfriends home; she shamelessly flirted with them even to the extent of sitting on their laps. Bill, an otherwise rational and intelligent guy, was of course taken in by her and believed everything she said because he was blindly in love with her daughter.

When Mrs. Thornberry learned Jennifer was not eligible to go to the prom, she went to the school and complained to Mr. Slack. She did not have enough charm to move Mr. Slack to change his mind. Bill had to take someone else as a friendly date. When something prevented a junior or senior from taking their steady boyfriend or girlfriend to the prom, a date with a friend was arranged. That friend for Bill was Mary Huff, a senior, who was dating a guy in the Army who could not get a leave to come home for the prom. We double dated in my car. Both of them stayed true to their steadies. As my date and I sat kissing in the front seat, they sat in the back seat barely touching each other and staring straight ahead.

The time line for asking dates to the prom was also well established. Four to five weeks before the prom was when people who were going steady or dating seriously asked their partner to go to the prom. In the fourth week before the prom, people who were casually dating and very attractive people began to ask each other, but those were easy decisions.

Three weeks before the prom, the weekly Hi-Teen dance became intense and there was a feeling of electricity in the hallways at school because everyone knew who was eligible to ask someone to the prom and who was anxious to go to the prom. People began to look at each other in a somewhat different light as they evaluated potential prom dates. Things like an irritating horse laugh, bad hair, a big nose, or even bad breath suddenly did not seem so bad when weighed against not going to the prom. Judy Jackson was in constant demand, because she kept an up-to-the-minute mental list of who was still available. This was the time period when junior and senior girls who decided they were not going to be asked began to ask boys from other high schools or older guys who were out of high school.

Two weeks before the prom was when juniors and seniors without dates began to panic. Their thinking shifted from finding that perfect date for the most wonderful night to just finding anyone to go with. Boys began to look at the girls they had never even noticed before in their Sunday school classes. Junior and senior girls began to look over the sophomore boys. Prom dates were often difficult for senior girls, particularly senior girls who had dated older boys who had graduated or senior girls who had not dated much and did not have a pool of potential dates. In Newell, Judy was on top of the situation. In the two weeks before the prom she was at her most effective. She paired up lonely senior girls with sophomore boys who had good manners and could dance, or shy junior boys with the sophomore or freshman girls of their dreams. She would approach kids in the hall between classes and bluntly ask, "If so-and-so asked you to go to the prom, would you go with them?" Having Judy Jackson freed us from the indignities of getting prom dates that went on in other schools like Chester High School, where the senior girls who did not have prom dates got together and decided which girl should ask which sophomore boy.

Less than one week pre-prom was the desperation zone, because it would be difficult, but not impossible for a girl to find a prom dress. At this point there were always a couple of people who desperately wanted to go to the prom but were struggling to find a date, and had seemingly exhausted all possibilities.

The most difficult match occurred in 1961, when the junior class president did not have a date for the prom. She had a number of strikes against her. She was very smart and ended up as the class valedictorian. She was very tall so she could not ask a sophomore boy who was short, she had some serious braces on her teeth, and as far as any of us knew, she had never had a date. But the most daunting feature was that both her parents were teachers at the high school. Tall, exotic girls were not in style then. Most boys went for the petite, cute girls. When she went to college she had her braces removed and got a stylish hairdo. She became so attractive that boys followed her home from college, but that was a couple years down the road.

The potential prom date had to be tall, smart enough not to be intimidated, and most of all, willing to take her to the prom. Judy Jackson had graduated and was in nurses training in Wheeling so the senior girls scoured both Newell and Chester, reviewing yearbooks for likely candidates, but had difficulty getting anyone to agree to take her to the prom if she asked them.

The teachers, seeing her plight, tried to help, but of course they were so out of it they suggested that people could go to the prom stag. Time drew short and the list of eligible boys dwindled to almost nothing. Then, the week before the prom, the tallest and smartest boy in the sophomore class, who had not dated much, agreed, after some badgering by the junior and senior girls to go if she asked him. The deed was done. The girl and her mother drove to Pittsburgh on Tuesday before the Friday prom to pick out a formal dress. The boy, who had just turned sixteen, drove his father's Cadillac and the happy couple went in style. The story of the teacher's daughter was one of the extreme cases of matching dates, but in Newell it worked and everyone had a shot at having the most wonderful night of their lives.

Every boy who went to the Newell prom, and every boy who went to any prom in that area, dressed the same way. The standard and most accepted dress for boys was a white dinner jacket that everyone rented from Marvin's Men's Store in East Liverpool for five dollars. I always went to Marvin's with Larry Hutton, because he had a car and could drive us over. In addition, he was a regular customer of Marvin's so we felt Marvin took extra care with us. Actually he could look at us and size us up, but he did have us try on a couple of jackets just to be sure of the size, and to make us feel like he was really giving us personal attention. When we went back to Marvin's on the Wednesday before the prom to pick up our jackets they were freshly laundered and pristine white in a plastic cleaner's bag tagged with our names. We also purchased a black bow tie from Marvin for $2.50 the first year we went to the prom, but we carefully kept the tie and used it for every prom.

This outfit represented the height of dress-up for men in Newell. I liked it so well I wore the same outfit for my wedding in 1965. Even though Liz patiently explained that for our afternoon wedding I should wear a tuxedo, she could not talk me out of a white dinner jacket. Most of the guys in Newell would never dress that formally again in their lives unless they went to formal dances in college, country clubs, on a cruise, or perhaps at their son's or daughter's wedding.

Just before dinner on prom afternoon I washed and polished our family car, a 1959 DeSoto. We had a DeSoto because Newell Central Service, on Washington Street, located just around the corner from our house was a DeSoto dealership. Our DeSoto was typical of the big, powerful, streamlined cars of that era. It was huge with a 290 horsepower engine, a four-barrel carburetor, and a back seat I could almost lie down on full length, if I ever needed a nap in the car. The car was white with an aqua color strip just below its giant tail fins. My father let me use the car only two or three times a month for dates, but I got it prom night because it was a very special occasion.

I began to dress for the prom right after dinner. My white coat from Marvin's was ready and I already owned the rest of the outfit: white dress shirt, black dress pants, and black shoes. The really cool guys wore white, button-down collar, short sleeve shirts, and black dress pants pegged or tapered in at the ankle to twelve or thirteen inches, and white socks. Mom pressed a white, plain collar, long sleeve shirt for me, laid out my black dress pants with regular sixteen-inch cuffs, and a pair of my dad's black socks. My parents were horrified when I came down stairs wearing a pair of white socks I had traded for the black ones. They made me go upstairs and change, which I viewed as just another example of their not allowing me to be cool. But, because it was prom night, I did not seriously object.

When I was fully dressed and ready to go, my parents proudly took a couple pictures of me on the porch and in front of a flower bed on the other side of Grant Street. All of the neighbors watched. The older women, like Mrs. Bennett from across the street, clucked approvingly and their young daughters fell in love. I specifically remember that Kristen Bennett and her friend Karen Dement came out of her house and practically swooned. They were just kids, in eighth grade, but in three years they turned into beautiful young women who made me sorry I had not paid a little more attention to them earlier.

I don't think the attention the women paid me was because I looked excessively dashing or handsome. I think I reminded Mrs. Bennett of her husband, Bob, and how he looked on the most wonderful night in her life only fifteen years before. To Kirsten and Karen I was a foreshadowing of the dates that they would have in two years when they would go to the prom. That night they did not see me as Bobby Barnett, from Grant Street, but as the personification of the prom ritual in Newell.

Going to the prom in Newell was not a cheap date. We did not have to buy tickets because of the fundraising activities, and nobody ever rented a limo or did any of the other extravagant things that kids do today. But renting a white dinner jacket, buying the corsage for my date, which cost either $5.00 or $7.50 at Riverview Florists, and spending $3.00 or $4.00 for breakfast was a chunk of money for me, because I got only $2.00 a week allowance. I had to dip into my college savings account at the Hancock Federal Savings and

Loan from the money I had saved while working in the summers. The twenty dollars that I withdrew seemed pretty significant at the time. The prom cost even more for the girls because girls' formals were very expensive and they were worn only once or twice at the most.

⸻

Prom week was always hectic with picking up dinner jackets and corsages and washing the car, but it was even worse for the juniors because they had only three days to decorate the gym. The Newell proms were always held in the high school gym, and a lot of decoration and crepe paper were needed to transform it into that year's prom theme. The decorating process began in February when the decorating committee began to meet and discuss possible themes for the prom and how the decorations would carry out those themes. The committee would then present its ideas to the whole junior class for a vote. Two years before, in 1958, the prom theme was Twilight Time because of the Platters' hit song of the same name. That was a great theme. Unfortunately, there were no good prom theme songs in 1960. The decorating committee recommended Cinderella's Castle as the theme and the old standard, "Some Day My Prince Will Come" as our song.

Most of the class didn't like that theme, so the debate was hot. The decorating committee carried the day when they pointed out that we could buy a complete kit with the materials needed to decorate a gym to look like the castle for $96. The kit seemed to be an easy way to decorate and no one could think of any better themes.

The castle kit arrived at the school two weeks before the prom. When Mrs. Schilling, the junior class sponsor, brought it into the English 11 class, we could not believe what we saw. The entire kit consisted of two small boxes of crepe paper with very vague directions. Rolls of light blue and light lavender crepe paper were labeled "false ceiling" with the instructions, "cut into two-inch streamers, alternate and hang over wires for pretend ceiling." An eighteen-inch roll of paper printed with what looked like a stone wall design had the instructions, "use to make a stone wall." The table coverings that were promised in the ad turned out to be two giant rolls of paper that had to be cut to fit the tables. There were equally obscure directions for covering the basketball baskets and decorating a throne for the prom queen and her court. I wanted to cry because of the impossibility of the task facing us and the inadequacy of the decoration kit. I thought I did hear a muffled sob, but when I looked through the room I just saw my classmates staring speechless in shock, although Deloris Grimm did have her head down on her desk.

Decorating the gym for the prom in Newell was a huge task that took the entire junior class three full days and nights. Decorating for the prom marked the end of our junior year in high school. It was our class's best opportunity to demonstrate our creativity and style. Our prom had to be, if not better than, at least as good as the ones before ours.

We started on Tuesday night at 6:30 for the Friday night prom. We spent the first half hour fighting among ourselves and messing around, because we had no idea where to begin and were overwhelmed with the whole experience. Deep in my heart I was thinking that maybe my classmates and I did not have what it took to be juniors and to put on a prom. I think the rest of the class felt the same way, but they tried to cover it up with crude horseplay and arguing.

Mrs. Schilling, our class sponsor, arrived at 7:00 with her husband and things started to turn around. They both pitched in and got us started on small projects. Mr. Schilling found hooks on the wall and began to string the wire we would use to make the false ceiling. Gary Evans, Glen Phillips, and Tom Woods worked with him on the ceiling because they were tall. Denise Bowen and some of the girls began to cut and stack the table covers. Dixie Miller, Edna Mehaffey, and Mary Nease started to work on the throne using risers from the choir. Clifford Arnett, who was kind of quiet and always in the background, turned out to be really good at figuring out how to arrange the risers.

Joe Fuller and I studied the brick wallpaper. "How can we make this paper stand up like a stone wall?" I asked him. We studied longer. "Cement blocks," he said. After some trial and error we finally stood eight cement blocks on end on each side of the stage, stretched the stone wallpaper around the blocks and folded the top of the paper over the top. It did resemble an eighteen-inch high castle wall running the length of the stage on both sides of the entrance arch. At the end of the first night we had made some progress. Joyce DeBee asked me to vote for her for the prom court when we voted on Thursday.

The next day we were in the gym every minute that we did not have class. As we worked after lunch, I suggested to Mrs. Schilling we use the freshmen boy pages to play fanfares for the crowning of the queen because five of the six pages were in the band and played trumpet. "Do it and write a script," she said tersely, as she held the ladder for Kay Gatchell, who was decorating the basketball backboard. Mrs. McDevitt, the band director, wrote a fanfare and had the pages practice it that afternoon. She even arranged with Weirton High School to borrow special long trumpets that looked like heralds' trumpets.

On Friday afternoon we set up the tables, put the final touches on the decorations, and I had the pages rehearse the crowning ceremony I had written. The decorated gym looked a hundred times better than three nights before. I always felt sorry for the kids at high schools like Chester who had their prom at the Virginia Gardens, a building at an amusement park, or high schools that had their proms in country clubs, because the only decorating to be done was to tell the florist where to put potted plants. It did not create a very magical atmosphere and a prom decorating committee of eight people could finish their job in an afternoon. That did not seem like much fun to me. When Carol Nease Stomieroski later told me that decorating for the prom was one of the things that forged strong friendships among the kids in her class, I knew exactly what she meant.

When we entered the door to the gymnasium for the prom, we were overwhelmed. The light from the setting sun shimmering through the translucent block glass windows in the back of the gym gave the crepe paper false ceiling a beautiful twilight look. The low fake stone wall did create a castle effect. The thirty-five card tables we all brought from home and decorated looked like huge flowers. We had created a colorful, glowing fairyland. As darkness fell, the lights filtering through the false ceiling transformed the gym floor into a dance floor. Our class had come through again; it was spectacular.

We were not alone in our admiration of the gym; a large crowd of people had gathered to watch the couples arrive. They settled themselves into the auditorium seats to await the main event of the evening, the coronation of the prom queen.

My Mom and Dad, who had come to take pictures, sat with Nedra Delong, my Mom's best friend. Nedra, who had known Sharon Haddox and Sue Ellen Logston all their lives, and me for as long as I had lived in Newell, lived across the street from Denise Bowen and two houses away from Tom Woods. She was a prom fan, who attended every prom, but this one was special for her because she knew so many of us so well and because she had seen us grow up. There were many other people in the audience who knew us all as well. On this night they made us feel like stars. It was our moment to shine.

Ruth McCabe and Joe Fuller pose for one of many pictures before the 1961 prom. Ruth is wearing the dress her mother made for her after taking seamstress lessons for six months. (Photo courtesy of the Ruth and Joe Fuller)

My date and I waved and posed for pictures as we walked up the steps from the auditorium floor to the gym floor and passed under the archway through the stone wall. Ruth McCabe Fuller later said the high point of the prom for her was to look back as she climbed the steps to see how proud her family and friends were, particularly her mom, who had taken seamstress lessons for six months so she could make Ruth's dress.

The first hour of the prom began with some dancing to the Bob Hall Orchestra. They were the same six guys who played at almost every dance at Newell High School. The number of songs they could play was very limited and the way they played them made the songs sound strange, but our adrenaline was so high we didn't care.

The crowning of the prom queen and her court came promptly at 9:00. I had planned and written the ceremony with as much pageantry as I could muster. The pages lined up on the edge of the stage in front of the stone wall and played a fanfare on the borrowed heralds' trumpets. I announced, "And now for the crowning of the 1960 Junior-Senior Prom queen and her court." The pages marched into the hallway and returned, each with an envelope. "Each page will open his envelope and escort the junior attendant named in the envelope to the throne," I informed the audience. The attendants were always girls from the junior class and the queen was a senior girl, all of whom were elected by the junior class. The pages played a fanfare. Joyce DeBee was the first of six junior attendants followed by Ruth McCabe, Dixie Miller, Sharon Haddox, Delores Grimm, and Marlene Daugherty. The audience buzzed with excitement and cheered as each of the six names was called and the pages escorted them to the throne. Then a hush fell over the gym. On cue the pages played another fanfare and I announced as dramatically as I could, "The 1960 Junior-Senior Prom queen is Miss Susan Derda." The

Bill Moffitt the junior class president crowns Susan Derda the 1960 Newell Prom Queen. The Prom Court were, left to right, Ruth McCabe, Dixie Miller, Sharon Haddox, Delores Grimm, Joyce DeBee, and Marlene Daugherty. (Photo from the 1960 Newell High School Yearbook courtesy of Ruth and Joe Fuller)

pages escorted her to the throne where Bill Moffitt, the junior class president, crowned her.

My classmates and I were ecstatic. Everything had gone even better than we had anticipated. The castle theme turned out to be perfect for a prom, and the pages playing fanfares was a stunning touch that had never before been used in Newell. As they were leaving Nedra said, "That was the best Newell prom ever. It was just like in the movies." My mom agreed. Dancing until midnight, the junior class floated along on youth, love, and the energy of our successful prom.

Unlike Cinderella, the most wonderful night of our lives did not end at midnight; the after-prom party was yet to come. The after-prom party truly set the prom apart from ordinary dances and marked our entry into adulthood, for it began at midnight and lasted until five in the morning. Our parents, who put on the after-prom party in 1960, my junior year, hired a regionally famous rock group from Pittsburgh to play. The group played electric guitars at full volume and their first riff was so loud it caused the gym to shake. We were in awe because we had never heard music played that loud, so loud you could feel it. That night we learned what it meant when people said, "This place is rocking." We felt very hip and cool.

However, the after-prom party my senior year was even more memorable because it was held in the clubhouse of the Waterford Park racetrack. We were able to use the clubhouse because Tom Bell and his two brothers enrolled at Newell High School in January 1960, the middle of my junior year. Tom's dad, the general manager of the racetrack, offered the clubhouse to the junior class parents for the after-prom party for free.

Since the racetrack was two and one-half miles from the high school, there were very strict rules for travel from the prom to the after-prom party. We were told we had to line our cars up in a caravan and no one would be let into the racetrack if they were not in the caravan. The second rule was we were not allowed to leave the party early. If we did, we could not get back inside. We looked at each other blankly as these rules were being laid down. Our proms were really tame in the sense that no one ever drank, there were never any fights, and no one even acted unruly. In short, we were on our best behavior. My Mom later explained that some parents were concerned about us having sex before or during the party, because three or four girls had gotten pregnant and had not returned to school in the fall of 1960. Adults blamed the pregnancies on Prom Sex.

What a stupid idea. Prom Sex in the 1950s could be compared to an urban myth like alligators in the New York City sewers. Other than the girls wearing low-cut, formal dresses, access to sex was extremely difficult. Most teen sex at that time was conducted in cars, so I find it difficult to see how someone could manage sex in a car, with a girl wearing a formal dress with crinoline petticoats or a hoop skirt underneath. I know the old saying, "Where there is a will there is a way," but the logistics of making this happen were almost overwhelmingly impossible. I have asked a number of people who came of age in that era about prom sex. They all nod their heads and say, "Oh, yes, there was a lot of sex at proms." But when asked if they knew of any specific instances, they cannot come up with even one. I know of only one guy who ever admitted to having sex on prom night and he was one of my college roommates. He and his girlfriend somehow managed to get her out of her prom dress and have sex in less than thirty minutes in the back seat of his father's Buick Electra. Frankly, this was not prom sex, but just the weekly sex they had been having for a couple of months. The prom just happened to occur on their regular sex night. The summer after the 1961 Newell prom, a couple of girls got married and did not return to high school the following fall, but believe me, it was not because of prom sex.

An article in the *East Liverpool Review* described the clubhouse as "posh" and was accompanied by a picture of Mary Nease, the 1961 prom queen. The newspaper got it right. We had a buffet dinner in the nicely decorated and thickly carpeted dining room, and then we moved into the main betting area that was two stories high with a balcony lined with overstuffed leather couches. Because I had worked at the racetrack for two summers, I had been in the clubhouse on numerous occasions, but the rest of the kids were really impressed.

The entertainment that year was a group of white boys in blue blazers from East Liverpool who sang close harmony. They had cut a couple of records, but were pretty tame compared with the loud rockers from the year before. After their one-hour concert, we danced until 5:00 a.m. to records spun by a disc jockey that came all the way from Akron, Ohio.

When the after-prom party ended, most of the kids went for breakfast at the Timber Lanes, a bowling alley about forty-five minutes away near Youngstown, Ohio. It may seem dumb to go to a bowling alley for food, but the restaurant in the back of Timber Lanes was actually very good. Liz, Bill, Mary, and I did not want to drive that far so we giggled over a late-night breakfast at an all-night diner in East Liverpool. There was no reason to be eating since we had just eaten four hours before, but the breakfast kept the evening alive for another hour.

After dropping off Mary and Bill, I took Liz home to Chester. Just as we pulled into the curb across the street from her house, the first grey shades of daylight began to appear. We sat in front of her house kissing in the car as it got lighter and lighter. Her mother, who was a crack-of-dawn riser, was "shocked to see my daughter sitting in a car in front of her house kissing a boy in broad daylight." At least that is how Liz quoted her mother, who became just one more mother who eyed me suspiciously when I showed up to take her daughter out on dates.

But, I had passed the prom test. Graduation, a summer job in the pottery, college, and my future lay ahead.

Epilogue

When the class of 1961 graduated from Newell High School, we were a very different generation from our parents. They couldn't wait to come home after the war and wanted to live in Newell forever. We wanted to get away from Newell, possibly to come back someday, but probably not. Ten of us, almost one third of my class, went to college. Many of the rest went away for some kind of vocational training or joined the armed forces. Part of the reason so many of us left was economic; the pottery and the brickyard were not hiring and the racetrack offered only seasonal work. In any event, we wouldn't have been content to follow in our parents' footsteps directly from high school into marriage and a factory job. We were raised in the optimism of the post-war era and had been steeped in the idea of meritocracy that was promoted in the post-war era by the G.I. Bill that provided veterans with money for college. We believed that a college education or some kind of training would help us to be successful in life. And we were restless. We wanted to experience the world we had seen on television. We became part of the mobile society that developed in America in the 1960s. It was easy to leave on the new interstates to find jobs with national corporations. Most of us did not return to Newell to live.

I was among those who left. In July 1963, my family moved to Columbus, Ohio, where Dad had been transferred by the Equitable Life Insurance Company. I had just finished my sophomore year at West Liberty State College in West Liberty, West Virginia, and in the fall would transfer to Marshall University in Huntington, West Virginia. Jimbo was about to start ninth grade and Janie would be a seventh grader. We had lived in Newell for twelve years. Although I loved those twelve years, I did not return.

⌣

If my classmates and I had come back, we would have found a different town than the one we grew up in. When my family arrived in 1951, Newell was in a golden age of prosperity and optimism. People sat on front porches on nice summer evenings listening to local radio stations and visiting with the neighbors. For entertainment, they watched the local teams or went to the movies in nearby towns once or twice a month. The town had a brand new grade school and championship basketball teams at the high school, the center of community life. The major employers, The Homer Laughlin China Company, Edwin M. Knowles China Company, and Globe Brick Company were all working at full capacity. Waterford Park, the horserace track, was scheduled to open in 1952. The town had a thriving local economy with eight neighborhood grocery stores, four bars, three restaurants, two gas stations, two convenience stores, a car dealership and an appliance store. Even though wages were low, everyone was working. We thought life in Newell would go on like this forever, and like everyone who lives in a golden age we believed that things would only get better.

We were wrong. By the mid-1950s things started to go sour. When the potteries could not compete with imported dishes from Japan, the smaller potteries in the tri-state area began to close. In 1962 Newell suffered a huge blow when the Edwin M. Knowles Pottery, which at the peak of its production had employed more than 1,300 workers, closed. Homer Laughlin was able to stay in business but reduced its work force from 3,200 in the 1940s to 1400 in the 1960s. There were no raises and few new employees were hired. Jobs got tight. Even the Newell High School athletic teams fell on hard times. The 1958 - 59 basketball and the 1960 football teams that I played on lost every regular season game.

Then things got worse. The heart was cut out of Newell in the fall of 1963 when its high school ceased to exist. The high schools of Newell, Chester, and New Cumberland were consolidated into the new Oak Glen High School, located in a rural area a bus ride away from any of the towns. Newell's old high school building was used for its middle school until 1992 when it too closed. Then in 2004, Jefferson Elementary School closed, leaving Newell with no schools.

Things got even worse for employment in Newell. In 1972, the Globe Brick Company with its 400 employees had been bought by the Combustion Engineering Company. By 1984, that company was gone too. Homer Laughlin was trying to get by manufacturing dishes and cups for restaurants but had reduced its workforce to 683 employees by the mid 1980s. The horseracing industry was dying. In 1981 Waterford Park lost $1 million and in 1983 - 1984 suspended operations for six months. Newell had an excellent chance of becoming a ghost town.

But in mid-1990s Newell's fortunes began to turn around. In an attempt to save the racetrack, the West Virginia Lottery Commission allowed Waterford Park to install 165 lottery terminals, which were really slot machines, at the track. The slots were a spectacular success. By 2000, the track, which was renamed Mountaineer Park, was so successful that it could undertake a $60 million renovation to enlarge its casino and to add a luxury hotel and a 4,000-seat amphitheater.

The Mountaineer Casino Racetrack & Resort. (Photo courtesy of The Mountaineer Casino Racetrack & Resort)

The Mountaineer Casino Racetrack & Resort, as it was renamed, continued to prosper and, with 2,359 employees in 2007 was the largest employer in Hancock County. That same year the West Virginia Legislature passed a law permitting table games like poker and roulette at racetracks in West Virginia if voters in the county where the track was located voted to allow them. In the June 2007 election the voters of Hancock County overwhelmingly approved a referendum to allow table games. When table games were fully implemented in 2009, Mountaineer expected to hire 700 new employees. The racetrack paid $3.3 million in taxes to the Hancock County Commission from its video lottery machines in FY 2008. In the first eight months they were in operation, the table games generated an additional $633,683 in tax revenue for Hancock County and the incorporated cities of Weirton, New Cumberland, and Chester. Mountaineer Casino has become a great source for jobs and is a huge revenue stream for county and city governments.

By the 1990s, the fortunes of Homer Laughlin were also

beginning to improve. Struggling to survive, the company had revived the production of Fiesta® tableware in 1986. As Joseph Wells III explained, "We had quit producing Fiesta® in the 1960s because the popular colors then were earth tones and Fiesta® used vibrant colors. We started producing Fiesta® again because Macy's and a number of other large department stores asked us to bring it back." The sale of Fiesta® took off and revitalized the company.

However, in 2002, just as things looked better, potential disaster struck. The Aaron family announced they wanted to sell their 65 percent share of Homer Laughlin. The company would have to be sold. At best, the new owners would continue to operate the pottery, perhaps under a different name, but on a much reduced level. At worst, the Newell pottery would be closed and Fiesta® would be made in China or Thailand where labor is cheaper.

Joseph Wells III described what it was like to offer the company for sale. "We invited the top five contenders here to Newell to put on a dog-and-pony show for them. After it was over my chief financial officer and my head engineer looked at me and said, 'You know, Joe, these people are just going to rip this company apart; they are going to suck all of the money out of it they possibly can and flip it and sell it to somebody else. Then the company is going to be gone as we know it. You have got to do something.'

"Well I can't tell you how low I was. This company was my life, it was my dad's life and to have this happen was just beyond anything I ever thought would happen," he continued.

By coincidence, Wells had dinner that evening with a friend who was the president of an East Liverpool bank. Wells was so upset that he unburdened himself to his friend. The friend quickly changed from friend to banker and, in that role, offered to explore the possibility of finding money for the Wells family to buy out the Aaron share. There was one catch, the two other Wells siblings, Jean and Elizabeth, had to agree.

Joseph Wells III, president of Homer Laughlin China Company with the company's best seller, Fiesta®. (Photo courtesy of The Homer Laughlin China Company)

Joe called his sisters and said, "Girls, I don't know whether this is going to be an opportunity or whether this is going to be a great big anchor around our necks, but I think it is the right thing to do. I would like you two to be involved with me and I would like to move forward.

"God bless them because they stepped right up and said, 'We have the same feeling you do about keeping the Homer Laughlin tradition alive in Newell, and we have to continue to do that if we can.' That is basically how it came about. I could have bailed out and sat at home, clipped coupons, played golf, and traveled around the world or wherever and not have had a worry in the world; but that is not what I wanted nor is it what my family wanted," said Wells. In a heroic effort, Wells and his sisters saved The Homer Laughlin China Company, the jobs of generations of pottery workers in Newell and Fiesta®, an American tradition.

Today, Newell is a study in contrasts. According to the 2000 census (the most recent data available) its population was 1,602, which is 499 fewer people than in 1950. The town is not aging well; it is still unincorporated, the streets still have potholes, and only a few blocks have curbs and sidewalks. The town has the same buildings and houses as when I left in 1963; they are just forty-seven years older. In 2000, the average cost of a home in Newell was $45,700 much less than half of the national average of $119,600. There are four small trailer parks that add to the town's rundown appearance. Yet, some of the houses sparkle with a fresh coat of paint and new landscaping.

Many of the businesses I remember are gone. The Shamrock Restaurant, which was built in the 1950s and served as a hangout for my friends and generations of Newell teenagers, recently closed. Fred Young's Market is no longer across the street from my old house. "We do not have any grocery stores, and we had eight when I was growing up in Newell. We have to go to Chester or East Liverpool if we want groceries," said my friend Bob Shenton, who recently returned to Newell to spend his retirement years living in his family home.

Yet, a number of small businesses remain and new ones have appeared. There is one local restaurant and a DiCarlos pizza shop, a regional chain. Newell now has the Northern Hancock Bank and Trust and the Nixon Funeral Home, two businesses we did not have in the 1950s. A new Holiday Inn Express Hotel, a Dollar Store, and a Subway restaurant opened recently just south of Newell.

Although most of the jobs in Newell still depend on table games and table ware, the area has developed a mixed economy. Four new companies are located next to what was once the Globe brickyard along a two and a half mile strip of land on West Virginia Route 2 between Newell and the racetrack. Steady work in a variety of industries can be found here at the Ergon Refinery (180 employees), Shell Lubricants (100 employees), Davis Distribution (40 employees), and C.E. Minerals Processing (35 employees). Few people are getting rich though; in 2000 the per capita income in Newell was $12,426, which was $9,000 less than the national average.

The Oak Glen High School football team, which plays its home games at Newell Field, is mired in a series of losing seasons. But the Oak Glen High School wrestling team is a source of community pride; it has won eleven straight West Virginia State Class AA-A Championships, and Coach Larry Shaw was named the 2008 National High School Wrestling Coach of the Year.

While Newell looks much the same as it did in the 1950s, the people have changed. Ruth McCabe Fuller who returned in 1965 to live near Newell and teach in the Hancock County schools after graduating from nearby West Liberty State College, said, "It is not the same, because we used to know everyone in town. Now I do not know half the people. There are a bunch of strangers living there." David Nurmi, Director of the Chester-Newell Chamber of Commerce said, "Newell is a transient community. Some people live in Newell and drive to Pittsburgh to work. Other people move in and out with the racetrack."

In the 1950s there were no strangers in Newell. We knew everyone and we knew their families. We even knew their whole family history. We all went to Newell schools and were taught by people who lived in Newell. Townspeople followed the school activities with pride, attending the sports events, the plays, band concerts, and even the prom. Everyone shopped at the same eight grocery stores. Almost everyone had at least one, if not both, parents working at Homer Laughlin, Knowles, or Globe Brick. Everyone attended one of the three churches in Newell or went to the Catholic Church in Chester. Everyone belonged to the same clubs, all of which put on the Newell Firemen's Carnival, which of course everyone attended. People sat on front porches and gossiped with the neighbors, and cared what the neighbors thought of them. People in Newell might have criticized each other, but they always stood together as a town and were proud of the achievements of their friends and neighbors.

Changes that began in the 1950s destroyed the feeling of small-town closeness that made Newell a wonderful place to grow up. Closing local factories, consolidating schools, centralizing shopping into malls and supermarkets contributed to losing the shared experiences and network of relationships that held the small towns together. Television brought the world into small towns and an increasingly mobile society scattered families and brought in newcomers who were just passing through. Like every other small town in America, Newell was no longer the small town that we had known and loved.

But all is not lost. On November 1, 2008, my wife, Liz, and I drove five hours from our home in Huntington, West Virginia to Newell for the dedication of a new Laurel Park on the site of the old Newell Park that existed from 1906 to 1914. With support from the Hancock County Commission, a number of Newell citizens had cleared the underbrush from the east side of the former park area, built a bridge across the creek, and laid gravel paths that followed the creek for about one-half mile.

The day was a beautiful, sunny, autumn, Indian summer day with just a hint of crispness in the air. The turning autumn leaves showed off Newell at its best. The dedication was held under a stand of maple trees brilliant with yellow fall leaves that reflected a golden glow from the setting sun on the crowd of thirty people who gathered for the ceremony.

We stood above the Laurel Hollow woods where I had played many times as a young boy. The ceremony was held next to Washington Street and I looked down the street to Newell's only stoplight that was glowing red and green. The old Newell High School building where I had gone to junior high and high school was off to our right. The world's greatest dump, now mostly planted in grass, was just across Washington Street. On the other side of the dump in the distance was the castle-like building of The Homer Laughlin China Company. Standing beside me was my childhood friend Susie McKenna Bebout. It was a classic Newell moment.

Sue Thompson, a member of the Board of Directors of the Newell Improvement Coalition, was the spokesperson for the Coalition. She was a good choice because she named everyone who worked on the project and even mentioned their children who came with them when the work was being done. The three members of the Hancock County Commission were recognized for their support and given an opportunity to speak, which they all did because it was an election year. The Wells family was also recognized because Homer Laughlin gave the Coalition a ninety-nine-year lease on the hollow. Jean Wells Wicks' husband, Victor "Pete" Wicks, spoke on behalf of the Wells family telling of the long relationship between the Wells family, the pottery, and the town. Following the ceremony the park was opened for tours, and volunteers served cider, coffee, and cookies.

Just as the group was breaking up the man standing beside me looked me over and said, "You're Bob Barnett, aren't you? I'm Ed Peters and I used to be a Newell postman. Didn't you live at 308 Grant Street, and wasn't your dad an insurance salesman?" I knew I was home.

Endnotes
for Chapter 3

↩

1. See Don W. Byerly and John J. Renton, "Geology," Robert Behling, "Appalachian Plateaus Province," G. Michael Clark, "Ice Ages," in Rudy Abramson and Jean Haskell, eds., *Encyclopedia of Appalachia* (Knoxville, Tennessee: University of Tennessee Press, 2006), 5 - 7, 8 - 11, 17 - 18; and Robert Mullennex, "Geology," in Ken Sullivan, ed., *The West Virginia Encyclopedia* (Charleston, West Virginia: West Virginia Humanities Council, 2006), 274 - 275. For a more technical explanation of the development of the Appalachian Mountains see Robert D. Hatcher Jr., "Tectonics," in Abramson and Haskell, *Encyclopedia of Appalachia*, 3 - 7.

2. Robert Mullennex, "Geology," in Ken Sullivan, *The West Virginia Encyclopedia*, 274 - 275.

3. J.H. Newton, *History of the Pan-Handle (sic) Being Historical Collections of the Counties of Ohio, Brooke, Marshall, and Hancock, West Virginia.* (Wheeling, West Virginia: J.A. Caldwell, 1879), 65.

4. Peter Siltich, "Mason-Dixon Line," in Ken Sullivan, *The West Virginia Encyclopedia*, 459.

5. Ruth Henthorne and others, *The History of Newell and Vicinity*, (NP: The Tri-State Genealogical & Historical Society, 1995 reprint), 11.

6. Henthorne and others, *The History of Newell and Vicinity*, 12.

7. Jack Welch, "The Homer Laughlin China Company," *Goldenseal*, spring, 1985, 9 - 10.

8. Jack Welch, "The Homer Laughlin China Company," and Jack Welch, *History of Hancock County Virginia and West Virginia* (Wheeling, West Virginia: *Wheeling News Register*, 1963, Revised 1992) 187 - 188.

9. Personal interview with Joseph Wells III, July 7, 2007.

10. Ibid.

11. William C. Gates Jr., *The City of Hills and Kilns: Life and Work In East Liverpool, Ohio,* (East Liverpool, Ohio: The East Liverpool Historical Society, 1984), 193.

12. Ibid.

13. Aaron Family Papers, American Jewish Archives, Manuscript Collection 621, http://www.americanjewisharchives.org February 8, 2008.

14. Interview with Joseph Wells III.

15. This was taken from a 20-page, undated, brochure published and distributed by the North American Manufacturing Company to recruit pottery workers to Newell. Held by the Tri-State Genealogical & Historical Society, Newell, West Virginia.

16. Henthorne and others, *The History of Newell and Vicinity,* 13.

17. Interview with Joseph Wells III.

18. Gates, *The City of Hills and Kilns: Life and Work in East Liverpool, Ohio,* 244.

19. *East Liverpool Review,* May 21, 24, and 25, 1909.

20. See, George B. Hines III and Lou Martin, *Images of America: Hancock County* (Charleston, South Carolina: Arcadia, 2006), 77 - 78.

21. Interview with Joseph Wells III.

22. Gates, *The City of Hills and Kilns: Life and Work in East Liverpool, Ohio,* 195.

23. Personal correspondence with Mary Nease Brindal, February 9, 2008.

24. Personal interview with Larry Hutton, February 12, 2008.

25. Personal interview with Marilyn Gibas, June 10, 2008.

26. This was taken from a 20-page, undated, brochure published and distributed by the North American Manufacturing Company to recruit pottery workers to Newell. Held by the Tri-State Genealogical & Historical Society, Newell, West Virginia.

27. Personal interview with Michael Martin, January 24, 2008.

28. Personal interview with Ron LaNeve, January 23, 2008.

29. Personal interview with Joan LaNeve Martin, January 23, 2008.

30. Ibid.

31. Henthorne and others, *The History of Newell and Vicinity,* 46 - 54.

32. Aaron Family Papers, American Jewish Archives, Manuscript Collection 621, http://www.americanjewisharchives.org, February 8, 2008.

33. Henthorne and others, *The History of Newell and Vicinity,* 87 - 89.

34. Jack Welch, "The Homer Laughlin China Company," 9 - 12.

35. Jack Welch, "The Homer Laughlin China Company," and Bob Huxford and Sharon Huxford, *Collectors' Encyclopedia of Fiesta,* (9th edition), (Paducah, Kentucky: Collector Books, 2001), 17.

36. Jack Welch, "The Homer Laughlin China Company," and Huxford and Huxford, *Collectors' Encyclopedia of Fiesta,* 8 - 14.

37. Aaron Family Papers, American Jewish Archives, Manuscript Collection 621, http://www.americanjewisharchives.org February 8, 2008.

38. Interview with Joseph Wells III.

39. Gates, *The City of Hills and Kilns: Life and Work in East Liverpool, Ohio,* 325 - 329.

Sources

Books

Abramson, Rudy, and Jean Haskell, eds. *Encyclopedia of Appalachia*. Knoxville: Tennessee: University of Tennessee Press, 2006.

Barrier, Michael. *Hollywood Cartoons: American Animation in Its Golden Age*. New York: Oxford University Press, 1999.

Bee, Clair. *Fourth Down Showdown*. New York: Grossett & Dunlap, 1956.

Barnouw, Erik. *Tube of Plenty: The Evolution of American Television*. New York: Oxford University Press, 1975.

Boyd, Peter. *History of the Northern West Virginia Panhandle*. Topeka, Kansas: Historical Publishing, 1927.

Catsis, John. *Sports Broadcasting*. Chicago: Nelson-Hall, 1996.

Callahan, James. *History of West Virginia: Old and New in One Volume and West Virginia Biography*. New York: American Historical Society, 1923.

Conley, Peter. *West Virginia: Yesterday and Today*. Charleston, West Virginia: Review Press, 1931.

Corey, Melinda, and George Ochoa. *The American Film Institute Desk Reference*. New York: The Stonesong Press, 2002.

Cunningham, Jo. *American Dinnerware*. Paducah, Kentucky: Collector Books, 1982.

Dixon, Franklin W. *The Secret of the Lost Tunnel*. New York: Grosset & Dunlap, 1950.

_____. *The Wailing Siren Mystery*. New York: Grosset & Dunlap, 1951.

Frank, Reuven. *Out of Thin Air: The Brief Wonderful Life of Network News*. New York: Simon and Schuster, 1991.

Gates, Henry Louis Jr. *Colored People: A Memoir*. New York: Alfred A. Knopf, 1994.

Gates, William C. Jr. *The City of Hills and Kilns: Life and Work in East Liverpool, Ohio*. East Liverpool, Ohio: The East Liverpool Historical Society, 1984.

Gille, Frank H. (ed.) *Indians of West Virginia: Old and New*. New York: American Historical Society, 1923.

Glock, Allison, *Beauty Before Comfort: A Memoir*. New York: Alfred Knopf, 2003.

Gray, Pamela Lee. *Images of America: Ohio Valley Pottery Towns*. Chicago, Illinois: Arcadia Publishing, 2002.

Goodwin, Doris Kearns. *Wait Till Next Year: A Memoir*. New York: Touchstone, 1997.

Gonzalez, Mark. *An Overview of Homer Laughlin Dinnerware*. Gas City, Indiana: L-W Books, 2000.

Henthorne, Ruth, and others. *The History of Newell and Vicinity*. Np: The Newell Genealogical & Historical Society, 1995 reprint.

Hines, George B. III, and Lou Martin, *Images of America: Hancock County*. Charleston, South Carolina: Arcadia Publishing, 2006.

Huxfordford, Bob, and Sharon Huxford. *Collectors' Encyclopedia of Fiesta*, (9th edition). Paducah, Kentucky: Collector Books, 2001.

Kismaric, Carole, and Marvin Heiferman. *The Mysterious Case of Nancy Drew and the Hardy Boys*. New York: Simon & Schuster, 1998.

Knight, Eric. *Lassie Come Home*. New York: Henry Holt, 1940.

Leonard, Burgess. *Phantoms of the Foul-Lines*. New York: J.B. Lippincott, 1952.

MacCambridge, Michael. *America's Game: The Epic Story of How Pro Football Captured a Nation*. New York: Random House, 2004.

Moore, Barbara, and others. *Prime-time television: A concise history*. Westport, Connecticut: Praeger, 2006.

Newton, J.H. *History of the Pan-Handle (sic) Being Historical Collections of the Counties of Ohio, Brooke, Marshall, and Hancock, West Virginia*. Wheeling, West Virginia: J.A. Caldwell, 1887.

Polick, Terri. *Modern Fiesta 1986 - Present*. Atglen, Pennsylvania: Schiffer Publishing Ltd, 2002.

Rader, Benjamin G. *American Sports: From the Age of Folk Games to the Age of Televised Sports*. Upper Saddle River, New Jersey: Prentice Hall, 1999.

Reisler, Jim. *The Best Game Ever: Pirates vs. Yankees, October 13, 1960*. New York: Carroll & Graf Publishers, 2007.

Shepherd, Jean. *Wanda Hickey's Night of Golden Memories and Other Disasters*. New York: Doubleday, 1971.

Shirer, William L. *Berlin Diary*. New York: Alfred A. Knopf, 1941.

Smith, Ronald A. *Play-by-Play: Radio, Television, and Big Time College Sports*. Baltimore: Johns Hopkins Press, 2001.

Sullivan, Ken, ed. *The West Virginia Encyclopedia*. Charleston, West Virginia: West Virginia Humanities Council, 2006.

VanAuken, Lance and Robin. *Play Ball: The Story of Little League Baseball*. State College, Pennsylvania: Penn State University Press, 2001.

Welch, Jack. *History of Hancock County Virginia and West Virginia*. Wheeling, West Virginia: Wheeling News Register, 1963. Revised 1992.

Williams, John Alexander. *West Virginia: A History*. Morgantown, West Virginia: West Virginia University Press, 2001.

Works Progress Administration. *West Virginia: A Guide to the Mountain State.* New York: Oxford University Press, 1941.

Personal Interviews

Clarence L. Barnett, James A. Barnett, Lysbeth Arner Barnett, N. Jane Barnett, Susan McKenna Bebout, Margaret Bennett, Mary Nease Brandal, David Brooks, Martha Brooks Fenton, Marlyn Gibas, Doris Barnett Ficca, Joseph Fuller, Ruth McCabe Fuller, Robert Gracey, Cindy Miller Goad, Larry Hutton, Joyce Parsons Kreider, Opal Lantz, Ed LaNeve, Joby Young Laneve, John Laneve, Paul LaNeve, Ronald LaNeve, Gene Lytton, William Mackall, Joan LaNeve Martin, Michael Martin, Jim McDevitt, Anne Miller Mayerich, William Moffett, Donna Nalley, David Nurmi, Marsha Seeley Nurmi, Brian Peters, Ed Peters, Robert Shenton, Norm Six, Carol Nease Stomieroski, Wayne Swift, Jean Barnett Verner, and Joseph Wells III.

Periodicals

The Brooke County Review, 1998.
East Liverpool Review, 1909, 1952, 1957.
Goldenseal Magazine, 1985, 1991, 1992, 2005.
Sports Illustrated, 2008.
Wheeling Intelligencer, 1952.

Index

About the Author

Bob Barnett, a lifelong resident of West Virginia, was raised in Newell, West Virginia. After graduation from Newell High School and Marshall University in Huntington, West Virginia, he completed his Masters and PhD degrees at Ohio State University. Bob taught sport history for thirty-five years at Marshall University. He has written more than 300 articles, book reviews, research abstracts, and encyclopedia entries in publications as varied as the *Washington Post*, *Saturday Evening Post*, *Sports Heritage Magazine*, West Virginia's *Goldenseal Magazine*, the *Journal of Sport History*, the *Encyclopedia of Appalachia*, and the *Encyclopedia of West Virginia*. He was a section editor for the *Journal of Sport History* and the *Encyclopedia of Appalachia*.

Bob married his high school girlfriend, Liz Arner. The Barnetts are the parents of two grown daughters, Megan and Alexis, have two wonderful sons-in-law, and five beautiful grandchildren. Bob and Liz live in Huntington, West Virginia and Sarasota, Florida.

About the Publisher

The Jesse Stuart Foundation (JSF) is devoted to preserving the human and literary legacy of Jesse Stuart and other Kentucky and Appalachian writers. The Foundation controls the rights to Stuart's published and unpublished literary works. The JSF has reprinted many of Stuart's out-of-print books along with other books that focus on Kentucky and Appalachia, and it has evolved into a significant regional press and bookseller.

The Foundation also promotes a number of cultural and educational programs. We encourage the study of Jesse Stuart's works and related regional materials.

Our primary purpose is to produce books which supplement the educational system at all levels. We have thousands of books in stock and we want to make them accessible to teachers and librarians, as well as general readers. We also promote Stuart's legacy through videotapes, dramas, readings, and other presentations for school and civic groups, and an annual Jesse Stuart Weekend at Greenbo Lake State Resort Park.

We are proud that Jesse Stuart's books are a guideline to the solid values of America's past. Today, we are so caught up in teaching children to read that the process has obscured its higher purpose. Children require more than literacy. They need to learn, from reading, the unalterable principles of right and wrong.

That is why Stuart's books are so important. They allow educators and parents to make reading fun for children while teaching solid values at the same time. In a world that is rapidly losing perspective, the JSF is working to educate tomorrow's adults for responsible citizenship.